IF
IT AIN'T
BAROQUE...

$^{MORE}_{\wedge}$ Music History As It
Ought To Be Taught

DAVID W. BARBER

IF
IT AIN'T
BAROQUE...

MORE ^ Music History As It
Ought To Be Taught

DAVID W. BARBER

SOUND AND VISION
TORONTO

Contents

PART THREE: WORDLY GOODS

Author's Note and Acknowledgements

When I finished my little parody of opera history, *When The Fat Lady Sings,* two years ago, I thought I had done with the world of humorous musical history. After the opera book and its predecessor, *Bach, Beethoven, And The Boys,* I thought, there wasn't much more to say.

I was wrong, of course.

And so here we have *If It Ain't Baroque...,* which we might consider a sequel to *Bach, Beethoven,* but from an entirely different angle.

This fresh approach, of looking at genres rather than biographies, opened up a wealth of new ideas and (quite frankly) a whole new source for jokes. I hope readers enjoy reading it at least as much as I enjoyed writing it. Even more so.

Readers familiar with my earlier books won't need to be reminded, but for the sake of new readers I'll say it again: the historical and biographical facts presented here really are true. No fooling. (Or at least true to the extent that some other historian before me bravely stated them in print, so I won't have to take the blame. This we call research.)

As always, I'd like to thank the usual gang: illustrator Dave Donald for his great cartoons, publisher Geoff Savage and Jacky Savage at Sound And Vision for their hard work and support. And my wife, Judy Scott, for her invaluable first impressions and for tolerating a slightly absentee husband.

DWB
Kingston, July, 1992.

Dedication

This book is dedicated to my wife, Judy Scott (one more for the road), and to the memory of journalist and author Will Cuppy (1884-1949), who keeps reminding me how it ought to be done.

Part One
OVERTURE

C H A P T E R

A CLASSIC PROBLEM

S OME PEOPLE WILL TELL YOU there are a lot of different types of music in the world. But really there are only two: good music and bad music.[1]

Although it might be fun to talk about jazz music, or rock and roll or even Sudanese dance music, for the purposes of this book we must confine ourselves to what, for want of a better term, is now called "classical" music — by which of course we mean western European "classical" music.

As a descriptive term, "classical" is hardly accurate at all: strictly speaking, "classical" music should refer to the music of ancient, or Classical, Greece and Rome. And since we have very little idea what the music of ancient Greece and Rome might have sounded like, we're not much further ahead.

The term may also be used to refer to the music of the so-called "Classical" or "Classic" era, the period of music that falls between the Baroque and the Romantic — roughly 1750 to 1850, give or take a decade — and is exemplified by the music of Haydn and Mozart.

So if you want to be pedantic about it — and some music lovers just thrive on being pedantic — you shouldn't be referring to the music of Bach or Beethoven or Wagner or Stravinsky as "classical" music.

---

[1] I have an ironclad and absolutely foolproof rule for telling one from the other: good music is anything I like; bad music is anything I don't like.

But the problem is that no one's been able to come up with a better term, or at least a better term that people are willing to accept. Some people call it "art" music, to distinguish it from "popular" music — as if to imply that Bach shouldn't be popular, or that there's no artistry in the Beatles. Others call it "highbrow" music, or other terms that are even less polite. Any way you look at it, you can't really win.

So we're kind of stuck with the term "classical." (And from now on I'm going to stop bothering with the quotation marks, if it's all the same to you. They just clutter things up and get in the way.)

CHAPTER

REALLY EARLY MUSIC

MUSIC EXISTED FOR thousands of years before anybody had the presence of mind to write it down.[1] Before writing, music survived by being passed on from one generation to the next — father to son, mother to daughter, brother-in-law to second cousin — as part of what we now refer to as The Great Oral Tradition.[2]

Even Stone Age cave dwellers probably had some sort of musical tradition, even if it only existed as a series of inarticulate grunts or by banging together a few handy stones or bones that were lying around. (Some modern performers often look and sound a bit like Neanderthals. Maybe that's why they call it rock music.)

Later, music got more complicated and was adapted to suit particular occasions: music for wedding feasts, music for burials, music to bring on rain or to encourage the crops, hey-we've-beaten-the-bad-guys music or music to keep dangerous animals at bay.[3]

The ancient Chinese had a musical tradition dating back

---

[1] You really can't blame them: they weren't writing down anything else, either. Not even grocery lists.

[2] The Great Oral Tradition relied heavily on the fact that most people are blabbermouths. As a method of recording music it was clumsy and prone to misinterpretation, but you must admit it saved on paper.

[3] The bagpipes were used by the ancient Scots primarily to frighten their enemies. It generally worked, as it still does today. The Roman emperor Nero played the bagpipes, too — and look what happened to him.

a few thousand years before the birth of Christ, to before the Shang Dynasty.[4]

Aboriginal tribes in Africa, in the Amazon rain forest and on the North American continent developed highly sophisticated forms of singing, dancing and drumming that still exist today. Drawings inside the pyramids of ancient Egypt show us people performing on primitive musical instruments, though we have no idea what the music might have sounded like. (One of the earliest known written pieces of music appears in Egyptian hieroglyphics dating back more than 3,000 years: it seems to be some sort of lullaby. It just goes to show that, even back a few thousand years, it took work to get a baby to keep quiet.)[5]

But fascinating as all of this might be, it really lies outside the scope of this book. Sorry, but that's the way it goes. We only have room here to talk about classical music. (If you don't understand what I mean by classical music, you obviously haven't read this book's introduction the way you were supposed to. Maybe you had better go back and read the introduction before going on to the next chapter.)[6]

[4] Ancient Chinese music is built on a fundamental note called *Huang-chung*, found by blowing on a bamboo pipe of a certain length. You determine the right length by measuring the pipe against a bunch of millet seeds. Precisely how this works I'm not sure, but it made sense to them.

[5] And who sang this lullaby? Obviously the baby's mummy.

[6] If you've already read the introduction, please disregard this notice.

CHAPTER

THE BIG PICTURE

THE HISTORY OF western European music really starts around the fourth century, with the church music we call Gregorian chant. This began as a single vocal line and stayed that way for a few hundred years. Change came slowly back then.

It took a few more centuries to add more voice lines. The monks didn't want to rush anything.[1] The earliest two-part chants are known as *organum*, in which to the main chant (known as the *cantus firmus* or "fixed song") is added another voice.[2] *Organum* comes in two main types: *parallel organum*, in which the second voice shadows the *cantus firmus*; and *contrary organum*, in which the second voice moves around the first pretty much any way it wants.[3]

By the 12th century, chant and *organum* had become even more complicated, with as many as four voice parts, all based on a Gregorian *cantus firmus*. The best examples of this music come from two composers named Leonin and Perotin, who developed what's now called the School of Notre Dame.[4] Much of this

---

[1] An abbess named Hildegard of Bingen did more than her share of writing some of this music, but by and large it was mostly done by monks. They had cornered the market.

[2] The term "fixed song" seems to imply that at some point the song must have been broken. But in fact it's more like fixed meaning rigged, the way you'd fix a race to make sure your horse came out the winner.

[3] There was never anything called *simultaneous organum*. The church frowned on this activity.

[4] I always have trouble telling Leonin from Perotin and vice versa. But at least it was awfully thoughtful of them to have been born in alphabetical order like that.

13

Notre Dame repertoire is preserved for us in a couple of manuscripts generally referred to as W_1 and W_2, because most people have trouble spelling Wolfenbüttel.

Meanwhile, Europe was being overrun by roving gangs of troubadours, trouveres, minnesingers and other wandering minstrels singing songs about unrequited love and drinking and other dangerous pastimes. (They were dangerous because most of the love was directed at other men's wives. Maybe it had something to do with the drinking.)

As music progressed in the 14th century, composers of a new generation felt they were writing better than anyone before them, and in 1330 a man named Philippe de Vitry wrote an essay extolling the virtues of this new style of music, which he dubbed *ars nova*, or the "new art." He thought it was just the bee's knees.[5]

In the mid-14th century comes the music of Guillaume de Machaut (1300-1377), who's generally credited with writing the first four-part mass. Over in England, John Dunstable (1380-1453) was busy playing around with the sounds of thirds and sixths and early attempts at theme and variations.

Leaving the Middle Ages and turning to the Renaissance, composers such as Gilles Binchois (1400-1460), Guillaume Dufay (1400-1477), Josquin des Pres (1450-1521) and Orlando di Lasso (1532-1594) started a wave known as the Netherlandish school. (Some people — old fuddy-duddies, mostly — called them outlandish.)

Like the School of Notre Dame, this wasn't really a formal school with classes or anything — which at least meant you didn't have to pay tuition. They were called Netherlandish composers since most of them came from what we now call the Netherlands, or the Low Countries.[6] One of their most important innovations was the use of popular secular songs instead of Gregorian chant for the *cantus firmus*.

[5] You'd think being archbishop of Meaux would have kept Philippe de Vitry busy enough. Obviously not.

[6] It may be difficult to think of them as Low Countries when you find them at the top of the map, but that's what they're called anyway.

14

By the 16th century this routine had gotten a little out of hand and the church bigwigs were pretty upset. St. Charles Borromeo, the archbishop of Milan, collected all the church music he could get his hands on. Eventually there were 1,585 pieces and he didn't approve of one of them. But a composer named Palestrina (1525-1594) came along and saved the day, convincing the church that music wasn't so bad after all, as long as you wrote it properly.[7]

The 17th century saw the beginning of what we now call the Baroque era in music — what some music lovers like to consider the Good Old Days.[8] The old church modes were dropped in favor of the two main major and minor scales we still use today — the musical equivalent of Celsius and Fahrenheit, if you want to look at it that way.

Baroque music's usually pretty easy to spot: just listen for the strong bass line, lots of notes and everything chugging along like a steam engine. Composers such as Antonio Vivaldi (1680-1743) in Italy, Jean-Baptiste Lully (1632-1687) and Jean-Philippe Rameau (1683-1764) in France and Henry Purcell (1659-1695) in England are all important in the general scheme of things, but none of them can hold a candle to the true bigwigs of Baroque music, German-born Bach (1685-1750) and Handel (1685-1759). Bach in this case is Johann Sebastian, J.S. for short, the father of a bunch of lesser Bachs who followed in his footsteps. (Handel is G.F. Handel, for George Frederick, or George Frideric, or sometimes Georg Friederich. But whatever his first names, his last name was Handel.)[9]

---

[7] That is, the way *he* did. Palestrina's influence was so great that even to this day whole generations of music students study how to compose just like him, in a particular form of academic punishment known as species counterpoint. (The human species, mostly.)

[8] The term Baroque comes from a Portuguese word meaning "rough pearl." Originally this was an insult, referring to architecture or music that was grotesque or in bad taste. Nowadays no one seems to remember this.

[9] Or sometimes Händel. Or Haendel.

Bach wrote a lot of organ music, more cantatas than you can shake a stick at and a whole mess of big churchy stuff such as the *B-minor Mass*, the *St. Matthew Passion* and a bunch of motets. Handel wrote a lot of churchy music too (there's that little thing he calls *Messiah*), but also spent a lot of time writing operas, until he decided there was no money in it anymore.[10]

Baroque music is beautiful and inspiring, but it tends to be a bit heavy-handed. The next generation of composers, in what's known as the Classic era, went for something a little less pedantic and stodgy. The undisputed masters of this lighter, more melodious style are Franz Joseph Haydn (1732-1809) and W.A. Mozart (1756-1791), usually known as Wolfgang Amadeus. (And let's not get into an argument over the Amadeus. Just call him Mozart and have done with it.) I could mention the Rococo at this point, but I'd rather not.

They concentrated their efforts on chamber music and symphonies, though Mozart also turned out a few operas you may have heard of. (Haydn wrote 108 symphonies at last count, while Mozart wrote only 41 or so. But Haydn lived longer and his symphonies tend to be shorter, so he had the advantage on both counts.)

After Haydn and Mozart comes the dramatic, passionate music of Ludwig van Beethoven (1770-1827). Beethoven was the broody type, and it shows. He wrote only nine symphonies, but he put a lot more into them.[11] Beethoven also expanded the repertoire of the piano, with which Mozart had been tinkering until he passed on, and took the string quartet off in directions it hadn't expected to be going.

Beethoven's emotional outbursts ushered in the Romantic era of the 19th century, in which everything in music got bigger, more exciting and just generally louder.[12]

Romantic composers such as Frederic Chopin (1810-1849), Franz Schubert (1797-1828) and Robert Schumann

---

[10] Handel was nothing if not practical. In fact, he was practically a genius.

[11] Especially the Ninth, into which he put a whole bunch of singers.

[12] Longer, too, as anyone who's sat through a Mahler symphony or Puccini opera can tell you.

1810-1856) or even Johannes Brahms (1833-1897) generally knew how far to take Romanticism, but in its extreme form it led to the music of Richard Wagner (1813-1883), a German-born composer of large-scale operas who never knew when to leave well enough alone.

Composers such as Giuseppe Verdi (1813-1901) Giacomo Puccini (1858-1924) and Richard Strauss (1864-1949) continued to write big, splashy operas, but as the 19th century gave way to the 20th, some composers worried that maybe they were running out of things to say.

Igor Stravinsky (1882-1971) added powerful rhythms and many elements of jazz music to his compositions. With Stravinsky, you never knew quite what to expect next. Arnold Schoenberg (1874-1951) shook everybody up for a while by discarding the long-established harmonic system of major and minor scales for something entirely new, which he called *serialism*, based on a strict mathematical formula that created "tone rows" using all 12 notes of the chromatic scale.

The problem is that serialism looks better on paper than it sounds in performance.[13] Some applauded Schoenberg for his courage, but others felt he'd thrown the baby out with the bath water and worried that he was leading music down the road to chaos. Obviously, something had to be done.

Some composers pulled back from the brink by rediscovering musical styles of the past and updating them in their own way (kind of like rerunning old movies on late-night TV). Thus we have new waves of neo-Classicism, neo-Romanticism and even neo-Medievalism. (Obviously it's too early for neo-Serialism, but it will probably come someday.)

As to what happens next, your guess is as good as mine. Maybe better.

There you have it: a crash course in 1,500 years of musical history in about as many words. Whew!

---

[13] In fact, it sounds a lot like music written by mathematicians — which is probably not much better than mathematics done by musicians.

Part Two
SECTS EDUCATION

CHAPTER

CHANTS ENCOUNTER

IT'S IMPOSSIBLE TO STUDY the development of classical music without bumping into the Christian Church. There's just no way around it: everywhere you look, there it is.

Before the Christians, the Jews had lots of music: they sang songs by the waters of Babylon, and praised the Lord with all manner of instruments, including trumpets and timbrels.[1]

But it was really the early Christians who took the ball and ran with it, making up all the fancy names and thinking up all the obscure rules that make classical music the formal, stuffy pastime it is today. Before that, everybody just thought music was meant to be fun. What did they know?

Things got off to a slow start, but by about the fourth century A.D. the Christian Church really started getting into the swing of things, music-wise. A bunch of monks started off by singing psalm verses and other texts to simple tunes they called *chants*. Because everybody sang the same tune at the same time — or that was the theory, anyway — this was called *monody*, from the Latin *mono*, meaning "one." (Don't confuse monody with monotony, which is only a by-product.)

Chanting was a big hit in church circles, starting first in Jerusalem. Later the church moved its head office to Rome, just in time for a sixth-century pope named Gregory I to take all the credit for himself. Legend has it that God had flown down from

---

[1] A timbrel is like a tambourine, only without the go-go boots.

heaven in the form of a dove, perched on Gregory's shoulder, and dictated all the tunes to him, which is why we call it Gregorian chant. And if you believe that, there's a bridge in Brooklyn I can let you have at a really good price.

Eventually, an enormous collection of Gregorian chant was assembled and put into a big showy book called the *Antiphonar*. This was kept at St. Peter's church in Rome, where it was attached to the altar by a fancy gold chain.[2]

Some historians believe the real credit for developing chant should go not to Gregory but to the Frankish rulers Charlemagne and Pepin III, also known as Pepin the Short.[3] But so far there seems to be no move afoot to change to the terms Charlemagnian or Pepinian chant.[4]

This early form of music is often called *plainsong* or *plainchant* (in Latin, *cantus planus*) because that's just what it was: plain. No harmony and not much rhythm, just a short piece of Latin verse set to a single melodic line. It was like plain yogurt, without the fruit flavor. Monks sang it because they were told it was good for them. (Like yogurt, it was a simple form of culture.)

Different variations of plainchant developed in different parts of the old world: all the little countries and regions wanted to do things their own way. Thus we have Ambrosian chant in Milan, Mozarabic chant in Spain, Sarum chant in Salisbury, Gallican chant in Gaul and Old Roman chant in Old Rome. (Sung, presumably, by Old Romans.) The general reader won't really need to understand these subtle distinctions. It takes a real expert to know (or care) how to tell, say, Sarum chant from Gallican chant. To my mind, it's hardly worth the bother.

---

[2] Someone later stole the *Antiphonar*, fancy gold chain and all.

[3] I tend to agree. In my opinion, Pepin has been given short shrift in this whole affair.

[4] In addition to fostering the growth of church music, Charlemagne gathered a large collection of love songs, drinking songs and other secular music popular in the eighth and ninth centuries. This collection was later destroyed by Charlemagne's son Louis the Pious, also known as Louis the Party-pooper.

Each piece of Gregorian chant uses a particular grouping of musical notes called a *mode*. If you've ever had to play scales on the piano or some other instrument you'll get the general idea: modes are like scales, only more fussy and obsure.

Modes come in two general types, *authentic* and *plagal*.[5] The authentic modes are called the Dorian, Phrygian, Lydian and Mixolydian. The plagal modes are called the Hypodorian, Hypophrygian, Hypolydian and Hypomixolydian. As if that weren't complicated enough, someone later added a bunch more, called the Aeolian, Ionian and Locrian modes. Nobody pays much attention to them, really.

The modes take their names from the terminology of ancient Greek music. Most of what we know about Greek music, including the names of the church modes, comes from the writings of a fifth-century scholar, poet, politician and general man-about-town named Boethius. (His full name was Anicius Manlius Severinus Boethius, but he only used that when he had to fill out forms in triplicate.)

When he wasn't writing poetry or serving as prime minister to King Theodoric the Great of Italy, Boethius somehow found the time to write a hefty, five-volume treatise on music theory, called *De institutione musica,* or "About musical instruction."

In these books — and they're real page-turners, let me tell you — Boethius expounds on his ideas about what ancient Greek music sounded like. How he did this without the benefit of tape recorders, CD players or even a written score or two I don't know.[6]

Boethius and his ideas became renowned throughout Europe for the next few hundred years, which just goes to show you can fool most of the people most of the time.[7]

---

[5] Why the authentic modes should be more authentic than the plagal modes I have no idea.

[6] My theory is he made it up.

[7] King Theodoric imprisoned Boethius in 523 A.D. and had him executed a year later. But I think that was about something else, not the musical stuff.

Without getting into a lot of heavy-duty music theory here, let's just say that each mode had its own set of rules, which determined where the melody should start and finish and established a sort of theoretical hierarchy to dictate each note's importance in relation to the others. Like everything and everyone else, music had to be kept in its place.

The church modes kept the monks happy when it came to music: everything was orderly, logical (after a fashion) and governed by a complex set of rules that only monks could understand, since they were the only ones who went to school. This helped them feel superior to the common folk.[8]

By this time, by the way, music was being written down, using a complex series of dots, squiggles and lines known as notation.[9]

The earliest music was written down using only one line, but it was an 11th-century monk named Guido of Arezzo who thought of adding a few more, so singers had three and then four lines, called a staff, to guide them. (It took another 200 years or so before anyone thought of adding the fifth line we use today. As far as I know, there's been no talk of shooting for six.)

Guido is also generally credited with developing something called the Guidonian Hand, which is supposed to help you remember the notes of the church modes and their names in the system known as solmization, or tonic sol-fa. (This was *way* before Julie Andrews sang "Doh, a deer, a female deer ... ") Evidently, Guido never had trouble remembering which notes were which. "No problem," he'd say, looking at a new piece of music, "I know it like the back of my hand."

As with other aspects of chant, monks were some of the few people who knew how to write it down using the staff lines, so church music tends to be the only music to have been recorded in this way. Regular folks kept singing drinking songs or love songs and generally carrying on, but their music was still rarely written down. Like everything else, it all depends on who you know. (Or whom.)

[8] Monks were the earliest form of bureaucrat.
[9] They had tried it first with just the dots and squiggles, but it was the lines that really made all the difference. It's the same with coloring books.

From the single or monophonic line of Gregorian chant it was only a short step to the development of two-, three- and four-voice *organum* and other, even more complex forms of polyphony. Or, as music historian Alfred Einstein puts it: "The ancient world had, of course, often stumbled on the fact of harmonic consonance." But you have to be careful: if you leave your harmony just lying around on the floor, people are bound to trip over it and somebody might get hurt.

The whole concept of consonance and dissonance, or which notes sound right together and which ones don't, is a sticky issue throughout most of music history.

In early church music, the rules were established along strict theological lines: the only notes permited to sound together were the unison (a bureaucratic trick, since it's the same note), the fourth, the fifth and the octave. These were called "perfect" intervals, because they were thought to most closely reflect God and God's creation.[10]

Thirds and sixths, an English import, were allowed a little later. Seconds and sevenths were looked on with great suspicion and the augmented fourth or diminished fifth, or tritone, was called *diabolus in musica,* or "the Devil in music," and was to be avoided at all times.

Realizing they'd rather boxed themselves in with these rules, composers later decided that consonant intervals need only occur under certain conditions — basically on what we'd now call the downbeat of the bar, except this was before bar lines, and at cadences. Anything that happened in between was pretty much fair game. This made life much easier

As church music became more sophisticated, it became standardized into several forms, or *genres*, that were determined by the kind of text being set. (Don't worry about that word genre: just think of it as the musical equivalent of the make and model of a car.)[11]

[10] How they knew this is anyone's guess.
[11] Later we'll learn about Tudor music — which of course is different from four-door music, or even the hatchback.

The most important of these genres is the *mass*, the general name for a bunch of liturgical texts used for each church service. It's called a mass because, having so many words, it tends to be massive. Or maybe because composers who wrote masses came to be regarded as heavyweights. Or something.

Sometimes the mass texts changed for special occasions, one of the most common of which is the *Requiem*, or " Mass for the dead." Another important genre of church music is the *motet* (from the French word *mots*, for "words," because, obviously, that's what it has). In England, they like to call them *anthems*, just to confuse everybody.

Other forms, such as *antiphons, graduals, collects* and *offertories*, are simply fascinating if you like that sort of thing, but otherwise we'd better just skip over them here. Don't worry, they probably won't be on the exam.[12]

[12] Hadn't I told you there was going to be an exam?

CHAPTER

A WORD OR TWO
ABOUT MOTETS

ONE OF THE BIG problems of singing Gregorian chant, and later *organum,* is that after a while you tend to lose track of the words. This music can go on and on for a long time on only one syllable of a word and sometimes it's easy to forget what word you're supposed to be singing. (The technical term for a group of notes on one syllable is a *melisma,* in case you want to throw it around to impress anybody.)

Even as early as the ninth century, some monks had gotten around this problem simply by adding a whole bunch of new words to the longer melismas, so that every note had its own syllable. In doing this they created whole new pieces of music, called *tropes* and *sequences,* to help break up the monotony. (The most famous sequence is the *Dies Irae,* which shows up later in the *Requiem.*)

This practice, generally called troping, began chiefly as the work of a couple of monks named Tutilo and Notker at the monastery of St. Gall in Switzerland, and later spread to other parts of Europe.[1]

By the 12th century, the Notre Dame composers had thought of a new trick: by increasing the length of each note of a melisma, they could create a whole new *cantus firmus* over which to add a freely composed second or third voice, which bounced along in a little dum-ti-dum pattern according to one of several established rhythmic modes. (The rhythmic modes

---

[1] Notker's nickname was *Balbulus,* or "The Stammerer," which may have had something to do with it.

are to rhythm what the church modes are to melody: the monks just loved having rules to follow.)

Leonin (or Perotin or one of the other Notre Dame guys) would take this little three-part creation — called a *clausula* — and plunk it back down in the middle of a section of Gregorian chant as a contrast to the plainsong.

The creation of *clausulae* certainly helped make the chants more interesting, but then they were back to the same problem of losing track of the words. You just can't win. (Sometimes it seems like the whole history of music is one long game of people putting words to music, taking them out and putting them back in again. It's enough to make you dizzy.)

By the 13th century, somebody got the bright idea of adding a new set of words to the *clausula* section, creating what was called a *motetus*, or *motet*, which is the Latin form of the French word for "words." (The motet is sometimes also called *motectum* or *motellus*, but only by the really academic types.)[2]

In most cases, the words added to the third voice, or *triplum*, were not the same as the words added to the second voice, or *duplum* — which of course were different again from the words in the *cantus firmus*. How anyone could understand what what was being sung I have no idea, but it makes for an interesting effect. Sometimes, to be really clever, these different sets of words would even be in different languages, making what is known as a *macaronic* motet.[3]

Once in a while, composers would combine a sacred Gregorian *cantus firmus* in the tenor with another churchy Latin text in the second voice and a racy French love poem in the third voice. They considered this very naughty.

By the 14th and 15th centuries, motet composers had to

---

[2] Some historians will tell you that it's impossible to study the history of the motet without a thorough understanding of the development of the *conductus*. Obviously, I don't agree.

[3] Obviously, not just any old composer can write a macaronic motet. You have to be very crafty.

think up a whole new set of tricks to keep themselves entertained. (And sometimes their listeners, too, though you have to be really on the ball to catch on to some of the tricks.) The easiest one was the addition of a fourth voice, below the tenor, to establish what we now consider the usual four-part harmony. (Or what you might call a barbershop motet.)[4]

Of the many devices in their bag of tricks, composers such as Machaut and especially his successors Dunstable and Dufay were particularly fond of a device called *isorhythm*, a sort of early Renaissance musical version of paint by numbers, which establishes a rhythmic pattern for the tenor voice (and sometimes others). Dufay, who became a canon at the Cathedral of Cambrai, fired off a lot of these.[5]

Composers of the 16th century — Josquin, Lassus, Ockeghem and crowd — continued writing motets more freely, often ignoring the need for a Gregorian *cantus firmus* (which had become rather tiresome) or even using fragments from popular songs in the tenor instead. (Just to show he was a good sport, Josquin wrote one song, *Guillaume s'en va chauffer*, with an easy part for his patron, the notoriously tone-deaf King Louis XII of France, to join in. After all, Louis was paying the bills.)

Speaking of paying the bills, one of Josquin's favorite tricks in writing a motet (and also its secular counterpart, the *chanson*) was to use a text that conveyed his frustrations over never having enough money. After waiting and waiting for a raise that Louis had promised him, Josquin composed a motet using the text *Memor esto verbi tui*, or "Remember thy word unto

---

[4] Readers wishing a more complete discussion of the evolution of vocal lines are encouraged to read a more scholarly history of music than this one. There are lots of them out there.

[5] One of the cleverest of Dufay's isorhythmic motets, *Nuper rosarum flores*, written in 1436, cunningly matches the rhythmic patterns of the music with the architectural proportions of the church for which it was composed as a dedication piece. Of course, nobody in the congregation was bright enough to catch on, but it was clever all the same.

thy servant." Louis got the hint and Josquin got the raise, so he composed another motet, "Lord, thou hast dealt graciously with thy servant." At least he was grateful.[6]

Around about this time in England a separate tradition was being created. After Henry VIII had his little tiff with the Pope and went off to create his own church, composers in England obviously couldn't continue writing motets with Latin words.

But since it seemed a shame to waste all their hard-earned musical training, they simply wrote motets using English words and called them anthems. Henry thought this was a fine idea and even wrote a few himself, including a little anthem called *O Lorde, the maker of al thynge*.[7]

In the 16th and 17th centuries, motets kept getting bigger and bigger: they're longer and they often have more voice parts than just four, often using more than one set of voices, or choirs.

The English composer Thomas Tallis (1505-1585) took this to extremes with his motet *Spem in alium*, written for 40 voices in eight choirs of five parts each. No one's been able to top that. Given its complexity and size, and the 40 voices, Tallis probably wrote *Spem in alium* for some special occasion, most likely the 40th birthday of Queen Elizabeth I in 1573. This was dangerous on two counts: first because it was not politically (or theologically) correct to compose a Latin motet for the spiritual head of the Church of England, and second because it may have been unwise to remind Elizabeth of her 40th birthday. Tallis seems to have survived the incident, so maybe Elizabeth wasn't angry after all.[8]

---

[6] Josquin was probably still sulking over the insult of a previous patron, Cardinal Ascania Sforza, who was stingy with his servants but paid a small fortune for a parrot that could recite the *Apostle's Creed* (which is more than I can do).

[7] Spelling was never Henry's strong suit.

[8] In her later years, Elizabeth I lost all her hair and went completely bald. She had a whole closetful of expensive wigs.

Palestrina wrote about 500 motets in what came to be called the *stile antico,* or "old-fashioned style." They're just like his masses, only a little shorter.

Meanwhile, in Venice at the church of St. Mark, the Gabrieli boys (Andrea and his nephew Giovanni) were writing big polychoral motets for two or more sets of choirs, often with organ or brass instruments. They'd place them on opposite sides of the large St. Mark's sanctuary and let the acoustics bounce the sound all around the building. The Italian term for this is *coro spezzato,* which translates roughly to "spaced-out choir." Obviously that's what happens to singers who perform too much of this kind of music.

Composers of the later Baroque, such as Heinrich Schütz and J.S. Bach, further developed the motet (and, in the case of Handel, Purcell and other English composers, the anthem). They introduced whole orchestras of instruments and elaborate passages for soloists and chorus. Handel's anthems are big and splashy (though not as splashy as his *Water Music*) and sound a bit like dry runs for *Messiah,* which in a way they were. Bach wrote only six motets, but they're doozies.

Later 18th- and 19th-century composers as various as Mozart, Michael Haydn (Franz Joseph's brother), Mendelssohn, Schumann, Brahms and a slew of English churchy composers and even many in the 20th century have all turned their hand to the motet or the anthem, but you can tell their hearts weren't really in it.

"After J.S. Bach the motet declined," says Willi Apel in *The Harvard Dictionary Of Music.* And who are we to argue?

C H A P T E R

ACHIEVING CRITICAL MASS

T HE MASS COMES in two general types, the Proper and the Ordinary.

Somehow, this doesn't seem right. Surely the two types should be either the Proper and the Improper, or the Ordinary and the Extraordinary. But obviously no one thought of this back a thousand years ago and it's clearly too late for us to correct the situation now.

It's the Ordinary mass — with the movements *Kyrie, Gloria, Credo, Sanctus, Benedictus and Agnus Dei* — that we're most familiar with today, in settings ranging from Dufay and Byrd to Bach, Haydn, Mozart, Schubert and many others. (Actually, the *Credo* didn't show up until the 11th century. But let's not quibble.)

What we now consider the first movement of the mass, the *Kyrie eleison* "Lord, have mercy," uses a text in Greek. All the other movements are in Latin. Don't ask me why. It doesn't make sense to me, either.

The mass can also be categorized as either a High Mass or a Low Mass. This, despite what you might think, has nothing to do with the range of the music. (Nor its quality, for that matter.) In fact, only the High Mass (also known as the Solemn Mass, or *Missa Solemnis*) is set to music and sung on Sundays. The Low Mass is used during the rest of the week and is only spoken, not sung. You might say that the High Mass is the mass dressed up in its Sunday best.[1]

---

[1] It's important not to confuse masses with the masses, who are the ones listening to them.

The mass gets its name in a roundabout way from the Latin verb *mitto mittere misi missum,* which means "to send, throw, fling, release or dismiss." It's found in the Latin phrase *"Ite, missa est,"* spoken or sung at the end of the church service. Roughly translated, it's the church Latin equivalent of "Class dismissed." (Or, I suppose," flung.")[2] Another meaning of the verb *mitto mittere* is "to pass over in silence." Obviously that doesn't apply in the case of masses.

Composers in Gregorian times wrote many settings of the Proper, including many by those Notre Dame guys, Leonin and Perotin. Most of these — hundreds of them, in fact — are conveniently available in one big collection assembled by Heinrich Isaac (1450-1517) called *Choralis Constantinus.* If you're bored sometime you might want to take a look.

Isaac's an interesting guy: he spent about eight years as court composer to Lorenzo de' Medici in Florence and later did a little spying on the side for the Holy Roman Emperor Maximilian I. (Like most of his predecessors, Maximilian I was neither holy nor Roman, but he was an emperor.) At some point Isaac took the time to write a song that became his one certifiable hit, a little ditty called *Innsbruck ich muss dich lassen,* ("Innsbruck I now must leave you"), a tune later stolen by Bach.

But by around 1250 most composers had switched to setting the Ordinary, probably because the same music could be used for more than one Sunday, which made their lives a lot easier. (They knew a labor-saving device when they saw one.)[3]

At first, even these settings of the Ordinary texts were pretty haphazard. The *Kyrie* and *Gloria* might be set in the same style, or even based on the same Gregorian melodies, but different ones might be used for the *Sanctus* or *Credo* or *Agnus Dei.* No one seemed to worry much about stylistic unity. It was more of a salad-bar approach.

---

[2] Or, in the vernacular, "Take a hike."

[3] William Byrd (1543-1623) published about 13 of his settings of the Proper as late as 1605, but he was a showoff.

The 14th-century composer Machaut wrote the first significant four-part setting of the Ordinary, his beautiful work *Messe de Notre Dame* ("Mass of Our Lady"). After that, everybody started getting into the act.[4]

One favorite trick that began about this time was the *cantus firmus* mass. Like the practice of earlier *organum*, this involved using a previously composed melodic line, usually in the tenor voice, around which the rest of the music was composed. (It's rather like decorating your entire living room around your favorite armchair.)

At first, composers based most of these *cantus firmus* masses on fragments of Gregorian chant, especially ones appropriate to whatever feast day the church was celebrating. (for example, Dufay's *Missa Ave regina* or Josquin's *Missa Pange lingua*). All very good and proper, you might say.

But later, many of these same composers started using other material, even — gasp! — popular songs, for the *cantus firmus*. Dufay wrote a mass based on the chanson *Se la face ay pale*, and English composers such as John Taverner and Christopher Tye wrote masses based on the racy love song *Western Wynde*.

One of the most popular songs for such treatment was one called *L'Homme armé* ("The Armed Man"), which was used by such composers as Dufay, Ockeghem, Josquin and even Palestrina (and I'll bet he had a hard time living that one down). Even the Beatles later used it, for their song *Sgt. Pepper's Lonely Hearts Club Band*.[5]

Later, composers took to borrowing whole sections of polyphonic music, such as a four-part motet, and using that as the basis for their new work in all voices, not just the tenor. (The first step in this process came when "elements of the *cantus*

---

[4] Curiously enough, Machaut is not considered a composer of the Notre Dame school.

[5] Palestrina disguised his *L'Homme armé* Mass, written in 1582, by calling it *Missa quarta*. But those sneaky musicologists found it anyway.

firmus now began to leak out into the other parts," writes one musicologist, conjuring up images of an overturned coffee cup, or an overflowing diaper.)

This type of composition is known as a *parody mass,* a form of which the composer Orlando di Lasso was particularly fond, having written about 40 of them.[6]

The term "parody" in this case doesn't mean what it does today, in the sense of making fun of something. It really just means "borrowed." (Composers in the 15th and 16th centuries had a much more relaxed attitude towards plagiarism.)[7]

Sometimes, composers feeling especially inventive would make up their own *cantus firmus*, basing the musical notes on something clever like the letters of a person's name. The technical term for this is *soggetto cavato*, which is Italian for "carved subject," meaning a musical theme carved out of something else. Nowadays, we might call it a "smart-alec" subject.

This is not to imply that Renaissance composers had no ideas of their own. They had plenty. Josquin, for instance, wrote 18 masses (and a few spare mass movements, just in case), and although most of them start with some sort of *cantus firmus* (mainly secular, by the way), they are full of inventive twists and turns and lovely musical devices, so much so that you tend to forget about whatever material he started with.

Other composers wrote their own masses from start to finish, without borrowing material from anyone. Byrd wrote three beautiful masses, one each for three voices, four voices and five voices. Byrd, a methodical man, helpfully named them *Mass For Three Voices, Mass For Four Voices* and *Mass For Five Voices.* (But just to confuse people he wrote the four-part one first, followed by the three-part and the five-part.)

Palestrina wrote some 93 masses, give or take a few, and many of them are wholly original. This was especially true after

[6] Lasso also operated under the aliases Roland de Lassus and Orlandus Lassus.

[7] The publisher Novello, which owns the rights to Handel's *Messiah,* successfully sued the creators of the song *Yes, We Have No Bananas* because it sounds too much like the Hallelujah Chorus.

his little run-in with the Council of Trent, the Catholic church's attempt to take all the fun out of music.

Apparently, church officials had gotten all huffy on discovering that composers were using the 16th-century equivalent of Top 40 songs to write their church music. Some of the more zealous clerics were even calling for a total ban on polyphony and a return to monophonic Gregorian chant. (Funny how someone is always carrying on about "getting back to the basics." Some things never change.)

Palestrina's biographer, Giuseppe Baini, says that the composer, recognizing a threat to his livelihood when he saw one, dashed off a completely new mass just to show all the cardinals he could be a good boy when he put his mind to it, and that polyphony wasn't so bad after all. (And just to be on the safe side he buttered them up by naming it in honor of Pope Marcellus II, the particularly devout pope who had preceded the current one, Pope Paul IV.)[8]

Paul IV later fired Palestrina from the papal chapel because he was married (Palestrina, not the pope), but evidently not before relenting on the idea of banning polyphony.

Or that's the story, anyway. Probably Baini's version is far more fanciful than the truth, but it does seem that Palestrina and his compositions did have something to do with dissuading the stuffier members of the Council of Trent.[9]

Having saved the day for polyphony, Palestrina went on composing masses (and incidentally about 500 motets) and paving the way for a slew of lesser composers who were really just marking time until Bach.

"The Masses of Biber, Schmeltzer, and Kerll," says Willi Apel in *The Harvard Dictionary Of Music*, expanding the highway metaphor, "are landmarks on the road leading to Bach's

---

[8] Pope Marcellus died quite suddenly from not paying attention to what he ate, or at least to who was feeding it to him.

[9] Apparently none of them noticed that the opening bars of the *Missa Papae Marcelli* bear a striking resemblance to *L'Homme armé*, the song that had started all the fuss in the first place.

B-minor Mass." Here we have the image of the modern-day music historian as traffic cop: "Well, you just turn right at the Biber, keep going past the Schmeltzer and hang a left at the Kerll. The *B-minor* will be right there in front of you. You can't miss it."

The *B-minor Mass* is without question the best-known of the five masses Bach composed (especially since the other four are incomplete, containing only movements of the *Kyrie* and *Gloria*). It is also generally considered perhaps the greatest mass, and one of the greatest vocal works, ever written. ("A gigantic edifice conceived by the composer as the crowning glory of his life-work in the field of sacred music," says the Bach biographer Karl Geiringer, fairly gushing with enthusiasm.)[10]

The work gets its name because it begins in B minor. It doesn't seem to bother anyone — least of all Bach — that most of the mass is in fact in D major, with occasional side trips to A major and F-sharp minor. I guess all of that was too much information to fit on the title page.

Part of what makes the *B-minor* (or D-major) *Mass* so impressive, of course, are what Geiringer calls its "monumental dimensions." Scored for double choir, soloists and a Baroque orchestra including strings, flutes, oboes, trumpets and drums, the mass is clearly larger (and longer) than even the grandest of Palestrina's masses. It's unlikely that Bach expected his mass to be used in an actual church service. Even he wouldn't expect a congregation to sit still that long. (The mass is divided into 24 movements, and some musicologists have placed great significance on the fact that, in the *Credo*, the word "Credo" appears 43 times. I'm not sure what this means.)

Just to show that he knew his music history, Bach based much of the material for the *B-minor Mass* on music from cantatas and other of his own works, making it a kind of parody mass. (At least when he stole, Bach stole from the best.) And portions of the *Credo* use melodies from Gregorian chant.

---

[10] Bach himself, in submitting the first two movements to the Elector of Saxony in 1733, referred to the "poor composition" of his "slight product." But then, he was grovelling to the elector for a job.

There's no question: Bach knew a thing or two about how to compose music. Or, as Geiringer so glowingly puts it, "The majestic work abounds in forms of intricate technical mastery." (Isn't that what I said?)

Although their careers show remarkable parallels in other areas (or arias), Bach's great Baroque contemporary G.F. Handel composed not a single mass. But then, Bach didn't write any operas, so I guess that makes them even.

The Classic era brings us masses by Mozart, Haydn and their contemporaries. Many of these are lovely, though not incredibly significant in terms of development, except for an increased use of orchestral accompaniment and vocal elaboration. (One historian notes — with some scorn, I'd say — that most 18th-century masses display "a superficiality, and even a frivolity, which is quite out of keeping with the solemnity of the text." So there.)[11]

Mozart seemed to favor the key of C for his masses: he wrote three in C major and one in C minor. (And an early one in G major.) Of these the best-known is probably the *Coronation Mass* (in C major), K. 317, written in 1779.

Mozart wrote it not, as you might expect from its nickname, for the coronation of any king, queen or empress, but for the annual "coronation" of a statue of Mary at a shrine near Salzburg. (It's amazing some of the things that inspired Mozart to write music.)

Haydn wrote a dozen or so masses, the last six of them written to commemorate the name day of Princess Maria Hermenegild, the wife of Haydn's patron, Prince Nikolaus Esterhazy II. (Having to write music for the boss's wife was something of an occupational hazard for Haydn.)

These are beautiful works, full of tuneful vigor and dramatic word painting. Some spoilsports were known to give Haydn a hard time because they thought the music sounded

[11] Though it wasn't until the 19th century, this same historian says, that "the religious music of men like Rossini became what seems to us little short of blasphemous."

altogether too jolly. But Haydn didn't care: he hated being glum.

The next milestone in mass composition comes from Beethoven, his great *Missa Solemnis* in D major. There's nothing especially solemn about the *Missa Solemnis* (though it's not exactly chipper, either). Beethoven was simply being academic and giving the work its formal Latin name, *High Mass* or *Solemn Mass*. (He wrote an earlier mass, a little one in C major. But that was just for practice.)

Beethoven was supposed to have written the *Missa Solemnis* for the coronation of Archduke Rudolf of Austria as Archbishop of Olmütz 1820, but he missed the deadline (as he often did). Beethoven didn't even finish the work until 1823 and it was given its first performance in 1824. By then, Rudolf had more or less forgotten all about it.

Anton Schindler, who was Beethoven's secretary and later his biographer, tells of visiting the composer while he was hard at work on the mass. "Behind closed doors," Schindler writes, "we heard the master singing, howling and stamping his foot over the *Credo* fugue." It upset the servants so much that two of the maids quit that same day.

After Beethoven, the tendency was for masses to get bigger and louder and longer, with huge choruses and full orchestral accompaniment. (They became, in other words, more massive.)

Composers from Schubert to Liszt — even Puccini and other opera composers — took a stab at writing large-scale masses, although some others stuck with writing smaller ones. (Liszt wrote both kinds: a big, splashy mass for Emperor Franz Joseph when he became King of Hungary, and a couple of smaller masses, including a *Missa Choralis* that uses Gregorian-sounding tunes.)

The great opera composer Rossini, always a kidder, wrote a mass as his final work, in 1864. His *Petite Messe Solennelle*, or "Little Solemn Mass," is neither little nor solemn (though he gets one out of three: it *is* a mass). The title page describes it as being written "for 12 singers of three sexes."[12]

Rossini obviously hoped that the mass would help make up for the indiscretions of his younger years (he was 74 when he wrote it). Along with the score, Rossini wrote a letter saying, "Dear God, here it is, my poor little Mass, done with a little skill, a bit of heart, and that's about all. Be Thou blessed, and admit me to Paradise." My money says he made it.

Composers in the 20th century continued to tinker with the mass. The English composer Ralph Vaughan Williams wrote a lovely little one in G minor that recalls the Tudor masses of Byrd: it's for unaccompanied choir and uses melodies that sound like English folk songs. Igor Stravinsky wrote a tricky mass for choir and 10 wind instruments and, in 1962, the Austrian composer Anton Heiller even wrote one using Schoenberg's serialist techniques.

Leonard Bernstein's *Mass* is no ordinary mass: it's a big, Broadway-style musical theatre piece for a huge cast of singers, dancers, instrumentalists and narrators. He began writing it in the 1960s and it was first performed in 1971, even though the FBI was pretty nervous about the whole thing. The Bureau thought it was subversive.[13]

At the end of the first performance in New York, Bernstein kissed each and every one of the 200 performers — which is about as subversive as he ever got. Somehow I can't picture Palestrina doing the same thing.

[12] I know I've mentioned this before (see my 1990 book on opera, *When The Fat Lady Sings*), but it's just too funny not to repeat here.

[13] Hoping to avoid controversy, U.S. president Richard Nixon did not attend the premiere. Maybe he should have.

CHAPTER

DEATHLY PASSIONS

APART FROM THE MASS, other large-scale churchy works for singers and instruments include the *Requiem* mass and the Passion (and also the oratorio and the cantata, which will have to wait for another chapter).[1]

The Requiem mass, or just Requiem, is a special kind of mass, also known as the *Missa pro defunctis,* or "Mass For The Dead." Composers have been writing them almost as long as there has been written music (though not nearly as long as people have been dying).

The Requiem gets its name from the opening words of the text, *Requiem aeternam dona eis, Domine* ("Rest eternal give them, Lord." Or words to that effect.)

The text of the Requiem is fairly close to that of the regular (or Ordinary) mass, although it contains an Introit and other bits of the Proper. Usually the more cheerful sections of the mass — the *Gloria* and the *Credo* — are replaced by texts with a little more fire and brimstone in them.[2]

The most famous of the heavy-duty stuff is the sequence *Dies Irae*, or "Day Of Wrath," which is all about fire and torment and judgment and is meant to keep all the listeners on their best

[1] I haven't forgotten about the *Magnificat* but I'm not going to say very much about it. It's the one about exalting the humble and meek, which is probably why composers are so fond of setting it — especially the English ones.

[2] Masses combining elements of the Ordinary and the Proper are called *plenary* masses, in case you were wondering.

behavior. (It usually works, at least for a while.)[3]

After the early plainsong settings of the Requiem, the first surviving polyphonic Requiem comes from Ockeghem in the 15th century, although even this is a shorter version. Ockeghem just wasn't up to the full treatment. (Dufay had a Requiem somewhere, but he lost it.)

Requiem writing grew more popular in the 16th and 17th centuries, with composers from Palestrina to Lassus to Victoria churning out a few. (Hedging their bets with the Almighty, maybe.)

Probably the most famous Requiem of the 18th century is the one by Mozart. By now almost everyone knows the stories behind Mozart's *Requiem*: how a tall, mysterious stranger in a cloak came to Mozart's door and commissioned him to write a death mass, which ironically became the last thing the great composer ever wrote.[4]

Mozart may have been afraid the mysterious stranger was the ghost of his dead father come back to haunt him. (Mozart had a guilt complex a mile wide.) Another fanciful story — you may have heard of it — says it was his jealous rival, the court composer Salieri.

In fact, the mysterious stranger was a servant employed by Count Franz von Walsegg of Stuppach, who wanted to steal the Requiem, dedicate it to his dead wife and claim it as his own work. This happened all the time back then.[5]

At any rate, the Mozart *Requiem* is a beautiful and expressive piece of music, even the little bits written by his pupil, Franz Xaver Süssmayr. (Mozart rather inconsiderately died before finishing it, leaving Süssmayr to mop up the mess.)

Brahms upset the apple-cart in 1868 with his work *Ein deutsches Requiem,* or "A German Requiem," for which he threw out most of the usual Latin Requiem texts and used German

---

[3] Hector Berlioz used the Gregorian *Dies Irae* tune in his *Symphonie Fantastique* to scare the bejeebers out of everybody, not least of all himself.

[4] Biographer Otto Jahn tells us the mysterious stranger looked "grave," which should have been Mozart's first clue.

[5] Nowadays it's generally considered bad form.

ones instead. (He didn't go too far: he stuck with the Bible.)[6]

Playwright and music critic George Bernard Shaw had no time for Brahms, whom he accused of being "rather tiresomely addicted to dressing himself up as Handel or Beethoven and making a prolonged and intolerable noise."

Shaw didn't much like the Brahms *Requiem*, either. He considered it "execrably and ponderously dull."

Among other composers to have written Requiems are Berlioz, Dvorak, Verdi and of course Fauré. (The tenors and basses have a lovely bit of barbershop in the Fauré *Requiem*, crooning "Jerusalem" in the background of the *In paradisum* movement. Keep an ear out for it next time.)

Benjamin Britten's *War Requiem* rather cleverly includes anti-war poems for a chilling effect and in more recent years the English composer John Rutter has written a Requiem that's currently in vogue. Even Andrew Lloyd Webber, the modern *wunderkind* of the popular musical, has taken a stab at legitimacy by composing a Requiem.[7]

Other composers, of course, wouldn't be caught dead writing Requiems.

*

Passions became most popular in the 18th century but are generally ignored today. That's in the musical sense, anyway, which is quite another matter from anything else. If you're interested in some other kind of passion, you'd better look in a different book.[8]

Choral settings of the story of Christ's crucifixion, or Passions, are an important tradition in both the Catholic and Protestant churches, as a musical representation of the centrepiece of Christian theology.[9]

---

[6] Brahms conducted an early version of his *Requiem* on Good Friday 1867. This happened to be April 1, though nobody thought of it as a joke.

[7] But I, for one, am not falling for it.

[8] I'd be happy to recommend a few.

[9] The Devil, wrote Luther in a letter to composer Ludwig Senfl, "flees from the voice of music just as he flees from the words of theology."

Passion settings have their origin in the Medieval tradition of the dramatic Passion Play, and also in Gregorian chant settings that date back to the fifth or sixth centuries, in which a cantor would sing all the various parts in different ranges of his voice. (By general agreement, the evangelist narrator is tenor, Christ is bass and the crowds are alto. I'm not sure why. Maybe Christ was actually a baritone. Who knows?)[10]

A 15th-century English composer named Richard Davy is generally credited with writing the first polyphonic setting of the Passion using a Gospel narrative (he chose Matthew), and soon such 16th-century composers as Lassus, Victoria and Byrd had jumped on the bandwagon, followed in the next century by composers such as Heinrich Schütz (who managed Passions of Matthew, Luke and John but somehow forgot Mark).

Passion settings in the 18th-century include the *St Mark Passion* of Johann Kuhnau and the *St. Matthew Passion* of Johann Kühnhausen.[11]

Reinhard Keiser (1674-1739) was primarily an opera composer, so in his Passion settings he went for dramatic effect. You can tell just by looking at the titles, which include *The Bleeding And Dying Jesus; Weeping Under The Cross Of Jesus; Jesus, Martyred And Dying For The Sins Of The World;* and *Jesus Condemned To Death And Crucified.* He wouldn't want you to miss the point.[12]

The greatest of the 18th-century Passion composers, as you might expect, was Johann Sebastian Bach, who outdid just about every composer at everything in those days.

[10] The role of the "most impious Jews," advises the 13th-century French theologian Durandus in his bestseller *Rationale Divinorum Officiorum,* should be noisy and harsh.

[11] I might mention the *St. Matthew Passion* of Johann Meder, but why bring that up?

[12] Handel, who played fiddle under Keiser at the Hamburg Opera in the early 1700s, obviously got the message. He later followed Keiser's example by setting his own version of *Jesus, Martyred And Dying For The Sins Of The World.*

Bach's Passions date from late in his career, after his appointment as cantor at the famed St. Thomas school in Leipzig, on the death of Kuhnau. (The job was offered first to Georg Phillipp Telemann and then to Christoph Graupner, but both of them turned it down.)[13]

Bach apparently composed Passion settings of all four Gospels, though only the *St. Matthew Passion* and the *St. John Passion* survive in their complete forms. (The *St. Luke Passion* is lost and the *St. Mark Passion* survives only in music he later stole from himself to use for a funeral in 1727. Bach didn't like to throw things away. He never knew when a piece of music might come in handy.)[14]

Bach's son Carl Philipp Emanuel Bach wrote 21 Passion settings (five each of Matthew, Mark, Luke and John, with an extra Matthew, just in case), but they haven't made the impression his father's did. It just goes to show: quantity isn't as important as quality.

[13] In considering Bach's application, a member of the Leipzig town council remarked that "since the best man could not be obtained, mediocre ones would have to be accepted."

[14] There is a *St. Luke* setting published, but most scholars think it's a fake. I'm prepared to take their word for it.

GREAT ORATIONS

WHEN THEY WEREN'T BUSY writing masses, symphonies, operas, chamber music or anything else, many composers found time to dash off an oratorio or two, or the odd cantata. (Some of the cantatas were particularly odd.)

For some, writing oratorios or cantatas was easier than for others, especially for those composers working before the invention of the symphony: writing symphonies takes a lot of time out of your day, and writing an opera can take simply *weeks*.

Oratorios and cantatas are a lot alike, really. Both of them use words and music to tell a story, usually something biblical or sacred (although many Baroque composers wrote secular cantatas, often for solo voice, and a few 20th-century composers — Stravinsky, for one — turned that around and wrote a few secular oratorios, just to keep people on their toes).

The term *cantata* comes from the Italian word *cantare*, meaning "to sing." So, obviously, a cantata is music for singing. But of course it's a little more complicated than that. (Isn't it always?)

To the best of my knowledge, the first person to use the term cantata was Alessandro Grandi, an obscure 17th-century Italian composer, and even he didn't get the spelling right: he published a collection called *Cantade et arie a voce sola,* or "Cantatas and arias for solo voice," in 1620.[1]

---

[1] Since he was the first one to use the term, you could argue that Grandi's use of *cantade* is correct, and that everyone since who's been using *cantata* has been getting it wrong — but don't hold your breath waiting for anyone to change now.

Early cantatas contained several movements, alternating arias or duets with recitatives and sections for chorus. They could be either sacred or secular, with words taken from the Bible, or from poetry written for the purpose. A cantata is generally shorter than an oratorio, although by the time Bach got into the picture somebody forgot to tell him.

By about 1700 the cantata had developed into a more or less standard form among Italian composers: it was generally a piece for solo voice and accompaniment (either keyboard, strings or small orchestra, depending on your budget), consisting of two or three arias connected by recitatives. Alessandro Scarlatti (1660-1725) wrote more than 600 solo cantatas for keyboard accompaniment, and another 60 or so for voice with other instruments (not to mention another 30 or so chamber cantatas). His son, Domenico Scarlatti (1685-1757), wrote only about 15 cantatas, although Antonio Maria Bononcini (1675-1726) cranked out 375 or more. (His older brother Giovanni Bononcini was the opera composer who became a big rival of Handel's.)

Cantatas never caught on very big in France, although composers such as Andre Campra (1660-1744) and Jean-Philippe Rameau (1683-1763) managed to write a few, just to prove they could.

Over in Germany, composers took a slightly different approach, preferring bigger cantatas for solo voices with full chorus and orchestra. Since they were used in church services they are called church cantatas. (The Germans tend to be very logical about that sort of thing.)

Heinrich Schütz (1585-1672) had gone to Italy and come back all impressed with the cantata, so he dashed off a few of his own, published as *Symphoniae sacrae*, in 1629 (and a sequel in 1647). The Danish-German composer Dietrich Buxtehude (1637-1707) wrote church cantatas that helped to inspire Johann Sebastian Bach, who walked the 200 miles from Arnstadt to Lübeck just to hear his music.[2]

---

[2] Well, not *just* to hear his music: there was the small matter of his eligible daughter. Anybody who doesn't know the full story behind Bach's 200-mile walkabout should read about it in my earlier book *Bach, Beethoven, And The Boys: Music History As It Ought To Be Taught*. I won't tell it again here.

As he did with nearly everything else, Bach took the cantata and turned it into something bigger, better and more impressive than before. Scholars generally agree that he wrote about 300 of these big, solemn church cantatas, although a mere 195 or so are all that exist today. (If you see any of the others, be sure to let someone know. People are looking.)

Interestingly enough, Bach rarely used the term cantata, except for the few Italian-style solo cantatas he wrote just fooling around. For the sacred works we call his church cantatas he used the terms *Concerto, Motetto, Dialogus* or sometimes just *Music.* But we call them cantatas anyway, just because it's less confusing that way.[3]

Not many composers after Bach bothered with the cantata, turning instead to oratorio, opera, symphony or just about anything else. Haydn did write a *Birthday Cantata* for Prince Nikolaus Eszterhazy in 1763, but only because the prince was his patron and he paid the bills. Mozart wrote a little cantata called *Die Maurerfreude,* or "The Joy Of The Masons," in 1785.[4] And such 20th-century composers as Igor Stravinsky, Bela Bartok and Benjamin Britten have written a few just for the heck of it.

Britten's cantata, by the way, is about the life of Saint Nicholas, better known these days as Santa Claus. If we are to believe Eric Crozier, who provided the words, young Nick was a very precocious little fellow who had a thing about water: he took to his bathtub right away and couldn't wait to climb up to the church font to be baptised.

Young Nicky was an impatient tyke all around. "Nicholas was born in answer to a prayer," Crozier's text tells us, "and leaping from his mother's womb he cried, God be glorified!" He probably wanted to look at his Christmas presents.

---

[3] Haydn didn't call his string quartets string quartets, either, but that's what they are.

[4] The masons liked it, which is more than you can say about their reaction to Mozart's other bit of masonic writing, *The Magic Flute.* Some people think they killed him over that one.

Britten's cantata is full of precocious kids: there's even a short movement sung by three boys brought back to life by St. Nick before the starving villagers can eat them. Timothy, Mark and John — called "The Pickled Boys" — are supposed to walk hand in hand down the aisle, singing "Alleluia." You would, too, if you'd just been saved from being somebody's main course.[5]

*

An oratorio is rather like a cantata — only more so. In fact, an oratorio is a lot like an opera, only without the scenery and costumes. Think of it as opera on the radio.

Oratorios tend to be longer and more elaborate than cantatas, and to perform one you usually need a chorus, some soloists and an orchestra. Oratorios are almost always sacred, most often telling some story from the Old Testament.[6]

The earliest oratorios, in the 16th century, evolved out of the liturgical dramas of the early Middle Ages. (I probably ought to say something at this point about the famous *Jeu de Robin et de Marion*, written by Adam de la Hale about 1284. But I'm not sure where to begin. Adam, born in Arras about 1230, was also known as the Hunchback of Arras.)[7]

Another important step in the development of the oratorio came with the growth of the popular Mystery plays of the 14th and 15th centuries.[8]

By the middle of the 16th century, a music-loving priest at the church of San Marcello in Rome named Filippo Neri began holding performances of small musical narratives in one

---

[5] The role is something of a tradition in my family: I myself was a Pickled Boy, as was one of my brothers before me.

[6] Composers prefer the Old Testament because it's full of fighting armies, raging floods and raining frogs. The New Testament doesn't have nearly as many nifty special effects.

[7] If he had been born in Notre Dame, he might have gone on to a promising film career.

[8] A Mystery play is not a whodunnit, like a mystery novel. Those weren't developed for another few hundred years, and have very little to do with oratorios.

of the side chapels of his church. This type of small chapel is called an oratory, or *oratorio* in Italian, which is how the compositions got their name.[9]

The very first oratorios were called *rappresentazione*, or "representations." They were set up as a dialogue between God and the Soul, or Heaven and Hell or some other heavy abstract concepts.[10] Palestrina and others of his crowd wrote a few of these, but the most famous, and among the earliest, is *La Rappresentazione di anima e di corpo,* "The Representation of the Soul and the Body," written by Emilio del Cavalieri (1550-1602) in 1600.

This work was what you might call a staged oratorio, since it did actually include some scenery, costumes and even a bit of ballet dancing. Some people even consider it an early type of opera. I say let them, if it makes them feel any better.

Music critic and part-time historian Richard A. Streatfeild, in his biography of Handel, is less than enthusiastic about Cavalieri's early attempts at oratorio. "The rudimentary oratorios of Emilio del Cavalieri," he writes, "differ but slightly from the operas of Peri and his fellows. There is the same dull waste of recitative, broken by no oasis of melody, the same slight thin little choruses, the same tinkling accompaniment." So I guess that means he doesn't like them.

By mid-17th century, composers had given up on staging oratorios and decided instead to concentrate on the music. This saved time, as well as money.

This is the period that produced oratorios such as Carissimi's *Jephtha* and others by Alessandro Scarlatti, who wrote about 20 oratorios in between all those cantatas, and Giovanni Baptista Draghi (1640-1710), whose 40 or so oratorios helped popularize the genre in England when he moved there from Italy to compose for the court of Charles II.

[9] Technically speaking, *oratorio* is the name of the part of the building and the works were called *oratorioni.* But that term didn't last long, so you needn't bother remembering it.

[10] *Rappresentazione* may be the earliest form of rap music.

One of the more colorful composers of this period is Alessandro Stradella, who served for a time as composer to Queen Christina of Sweden, and had digs in Rome. He was born on the outskirts of Rome in 1644 and died rather suddenly in Genoa in 1682, when something he ate didn't agree with him. (I think it was a knife.)

Stradella composed about 250 cantatas but only eight oratorios. He would have written more if he hadn't been so busy doing other things, such as having affairs with singers and with women who weren't, technically, available. Among the affairs that we know about are ones with the singers Pia Antinori and Giorgina Cesi, as well as with the "nun-widow" Lisabetta Marmorani.[11]

Stradella narrowly escaped a jail sentence when he was implicated, along with the Roman Catholic abbot Antonio Sforza and the violinist Carlo Ambrogio Lonati, in a scheme to embezzle money from the church. Antonio, being a church figure and a member of the powerful Sforza family, got off scot-free while Lonati actually served some time. Stradella simply skipped town to avoid any problems.

Stradella got in even more trouble soon after for having an affair with the mistress of Alvise Contarini.[12] He skipped town again, leaving Venice for Turin. Unfortunately, Contarini was mightily put out, so he sent a couple of assassins after Stradella. They made an attempt on his life in 1677, but didn't manage to kill him. (According to one fanciful story, they were so moved after hearing a performance of one of his oratorios — I wish I knew which one — that they didn't have the heart to kill him.)

Having survived one attempt on his life, Stradella wasn't so lucky a few years later. He was killed on February 25, 1682, in a market square by a soldier hired by the Lomellini brothers,

[11] I'm presuming she became a widow before becoming a nun. I think that's generally how it works.
[12] Her name, apparently, was Hortensia.

who didn't like the way that Stradella had been making eyes (and probably more) at their sister. Family loyalty was very important in Italy in those days. It still is.

Over in Germany, Baroque composers — such as Schütz, Buxtehude, Bach, Telemann and C.P.E. Bach — all tried their hand at oratorio, some more successfully than others. Bach's *Christmas Oratorio,* written in 1733-34, is probably the most important, followed by his *Easter Oratorio* of 1736.

But it was really Handel, that German transplanted to England, who developed the oratorio to its greatest height.

Handel first became interested in oratorio as a young man visiting Rome around 1707, where he composed a few before turning his talents to writing operas. (It was a short transition: he stole some of the music from his oratorio *La Resurrezione* and used it in his opera *Agrippina* a year later.)

Handel later abandoned opera and returned to writing oratorios in the last decades of his life in London. He just got tired of losing money on big, elaborate fully staged operas that flopped. (Handel, we should note, intended his oratorios to be performed during Lent, the time of the church calendar when theatrical performances were forbidden by law. Trust Handel to find just the sort of loophole he needed to be able to make some money.)

Handel oratorios of this period include *Israel In Egypt* (1737), *Judas Maccabeus* (1746) and *Jephtha* (1751). But of course the most famous oratorio of all time is Handel's *Messiah,* written in just under three weeks in 1742 for a performance in Dublin. Even in Handel's day it grew enormously popular, and it has since become a mainstay (some might say a millstone) of the choral repertoire.

Handel is a hard act to follow. With the possible exception of Haydn's *Die Schöpfung,* ("The Creation"), of 1797 and *Die Jahreszeiten,* ("The Seasons"), of 1801, the next significant oratorios did not appear until those of Felix Mendelssohn, *St. Paul* (1836) and *Elijah* (1846).

Oratorios of the late 18th and early 19th centuries, writes music critic and historian H.C. Colles in an early edition of

Grove's dictionary, disappeared under the "elephantine shadow of Handel." There were oratorios written between Handel and Mendelssohn, Colles says, but "their music is nothing worse than intolerably dull." So there.

It may surprise you to learn that even Richard Wagner composed an oratorio, *Das Liebesmahl der Apostel* ("The Love-feast of the Apostles"), around 1844. It certainly surprised me.

Oratorio enjoyed a brief revival in England in the early 20th century, with works by Edward Elgar (1857-1934) such as *The Dream Of Gerontius* (1900) and *The Kingdom* (1903), and *Belshazzar's Feast*, by William Walton (1902-1983).

Igor Stravinsky (1882-1971) has written a few oratorios, but his only confuse matters. *Oedipus Rex* (1927) is pretty clearly an oratorio except that its subject matter is secular, not sacred, and I'm not quite sure how to classify his *Symphony of Psalms* (1930), which isn't a symphony at all, but a work for choir and orchestra. Let me get back to you on that.

Part Three
WORLDLY GOODS

TRADITIONAL
BLUNT INSTRUMENTS

S CHOLARS WILL TELL YOU that musical instruments are divided into three main groups or families, called *aerophones, chordophones* and *ideophones*.[1]

Ordinary people know these as wind instruments, stringed instruments and percussion instruments. Or — let's be blunt about it — things you blow, things you scrape and things you hit. (Sometimes the scraped ones you pluck and the hit ones you shake, but let's not get into that.)

The percussion group, if you're going to be really pedantic also includes a category of instruments called *membranophones*, or ones that produce sound using a stretched membrane or skin. In other words, a drum. ("The mirliton," the *Harvard Dictionary Of Music* reminds us, "is a membranophone that is not a drum.")[2]

The piano, harpsichord and other keyboard instruments are generally classed with the strings (except the organ, which is a wind instrument). Some people like to think of the piano as a percussion instrument, since it uses little hammers to hit the strings. You could keep yourself awake at nights trying to

[1] The telephone, a more complex modern instrument, didn't come along until later.

[2] Look up *mirliton* in the HDM and it will tell you it's "an instrument consisting of a pipe closed at one end by a membrane." The sound of singing or humming into the pipe is altered by the membrane, says the dictionary, "becoming quite nasal." In 17th-century France, the mirliton was known as the *flute- eunuque,* or "eunuch flute." All of which sounds very impressive, but is really just a fancy way of saying it's a kazoo.

decide whether the piano is a stringed instrument or a percussion instrument, but personally I wouldn't bother.

Instruments can be played individually, in small groups called ensembles, or in big mobs, sometimes called orchestras.

In the early centuries of musical development, instruments played largely a supporting role — second fiddle, you might say — to vocal music. This was especially true in the church, where of course most of the vocal music took place. Church authorities generally took a dim view of musical instruments because instruments were often played by jugglers, actors, pagans and other second-class citizens.

In fact, there's evidence to suggest that musical instruments were not allowed in churches at all until well into the Middle Ages. This seems a bit odd, considering the number of times musical instruments are mentioned in the Bible, especially in the Old Testament. (See Gabriel's trumpet, Joshua's horn, those harps hanging by the waters of Babylon, etc. etc.)

It wasn't until the tenth century or so that any instrument became accepted as part of church activity, and even at that usually only the organ was considered acceptable.

In fact, the early Christian church wasn't even very fond of the organ. The ancient Greeks and Romans had an organ-like instrument, called the *hydraulos* or *hydraulus* because it used a water tank to create air pressure for the pipes. Credit for inventing the *hydraulos* generally goes to Ktesibios of Alexandria, who dreamed it up around 275 B.C. (Cicero thought there was something fishy about the *hydraulos*, but he liked it anyway.)[3]

The Greeks played the *hydraulos* in their homes, but the Romans, being showoffs, preferred it for public festivals, gladiator tournaments and other celebrations, the highlight of which sometimes featured feeding Christians to the lions. Later Christians, needless to say, didn't like to be reminded of lions

[3] What he said was it sounded "as delectable to the ears as is the most delicious fish to the palate."

eating their forebears, so they were reluctant to tolerate any sort of instrument, especially anything that reminded them of the *hydraulos*.[4]

Eventually, however, the organ became what Guillaume de Machaut called "the king of instruments," and the one most closely associated with church music. It just goes to show what you can accomplish if you really try. (Nowadays the organ seems a particularly appropriate instrument to associate with the church, being too big, old-fashioned and full of hot air.)

But outside the church it was a different story, as it usually is: there were instruments all over the place.

The percussion instruments probably came first, since they were the easiest ones to find lying around. (After all, all you have to do is bang a couple of sticks together and you've got a percussion instrument of sorts.) Next came the woodwinds, starting off with the simplest of hollow reeds. Many early wind instruments were made from hollowed-out gourds or whatever else was handy. (The medieval instrument called the *gemshorn*, for instance, was originally made from a goat's horn.) Later came the stringed instruments, initially using strings made from the intestines of sheep or other animals.[5]

The brass instruments, which are classed with the other winds, were the last to develop, not because the instruments themselves were especially complicated, but because the skills and tools for fashioning brass weren't developed until later. (Animal horns probably played a part here too in the earliest of trumpet-like instruments — which is why we call them horns, after all.)

All of which makes it sound like the development of musical instruments was orderly and logical, which of course it wasn't. It was nothing much more than an enormous hodge-podge most of the time, especially in the early stages. But

---

[4] Some historians now say there's no truth to the story that early Christians were fed to the lions. You can believe whatever you like. I'm not taking sides.

[5] Even today, musicians say strings are made of "catgut." But they're only joking: cats don't enter into it. At least not if they're smart.

somehow everyone muddled through.

By the middle of the Middle Ages, musicians had developed a huge collection of different instruments in each of the four main families. There were drums of all shapes and sizes, bells and gongs and all manner of things to bang or shake.[6] There were simple wind instruments such as the flute, recorder or the *gemshorn*, and ones that used buzzing reeds, such as the *crumhorn* (or *krummhorn*), the *dulcian* or the *shawm*. (The shawm is an early double-reed instrument — a sort of oboe, but even more obnoxious.) There were plucked guitar-like stringed instruments such as the lute, the cittern, the pandora and the guitar, and bowed stringed instruments such as the three-stringed *rebec* and later the viols.

The viol is a sort of forerunner of the modern violin family. Viols had a softer sound and came in different sizes, corresponding roughly to the present-day violin, viola and cello. But viols had six strings (instead of the violin family's four) and a slightly different bow. And each viol, even the small treble, was held on the lap or between the knees, the way you would a cello.

Eventually the viol family was supplanted by the violin, viola and cello, which became the instruments of choice among orchestral and solo performers of the Baroque and later eras. Viols are lovely instruments, but playing them can be a problem: there are just too many strings attached.

And last in the development of musical instruments there came the brass instruments, from the simplest straight trumpets (those long things the heralds play in old Hollywood Robin Hood movies) to an instrument with the unlikely name of the *sackbut,* a sort of glorified slide-whistle and the forerunner of the modern trombone.

Historian Francis Galpin says the name sackbut comes from the Spanish term *sacabuche* or *saquebute,* meaning "draw-trumpet," whereas musicologist Curt Sachs says it comes from the French *saqueboute*, combining *saquer* (to pull) and *bouter* (to

---

[6] Early drums were often called *tabors*, but they amount to the same thing.

push). Far be it from me to argue with such accomplished scholars. Wherever the term came from, the English seemed to have a hard time with the name, calling it, among other things, *seykebuds, sakbuds, shagbolt, shagbutts* and even *shakebuttes*.[7]

Another oddly named medieval instrument is the hurdy-gurdy, a stringed instrument you play by turning a handcrank. And the *tromba marina,* despite its name, is not a trumpet and has nothing to do with boats or the water.

Medieval musicians divided their instruments into two main categories: there were "outdoor" instruments and "indoor" instruments. Mostly this had to do with volume: the really loud ones you played outdoors for pageants and battles, and the quieter ones you played indoors for feasts and other entertainments.[8]

But even within those two broad categories there were hundreds of variations. Instruments came in all sizes and shapes, since they tended to be made with whatever materials were available. (You try getting a goat to grow horns exactly the right size. It isn't easy: goats are stubborn.)

The result, depending on how you look at it, was either a fascinating array of sounds from an enormous variety of instruments or a monstrous jumble of odd-shaped noisemakers. (At his death in 1547, King Henry VIII of England, who was very fond of music, left a collection of instruments that included 76 recorders, 72 flutes, 25 shawms, 25 crumhorns, 11 fifes, 23 virginals, 15 regals, two clavichords, 12 violins, five guitars, two cornets, 26 lutes and five bagpipes. And a partridge in a pear tree.)[9]

The resulting sound from all these instruments is what musicologists like to call *heterogeneous,* a fancy term that comes

[7] As to how to pronounce the *crwth,* a kind of Celtic lyre, you're on your own.

[8] Oddly enough, despite its name, the indoor wind instrument called the *rackett* — a forerunner of the modern bassoon about the size and shape of a coffee can — has a sound that's actually quite soft and sweet. Go figure.

[9] Some sources say 13 crumhorns, 31 virginals and 78 recorders and so on, but you get the idea: a whole lot of instruments.

from a Greek word meaning "diverse." (Try throwing it around at your next dinner party and see what happens.)

This diversity of musical instruments and sounds came partly because each instrument maker did things his own way, and partly because musicians had established no form of standard pitch, by which modern players get in tune with each other.

In the Middle Ages, musicians playing together at a certain court or in a certain town might have some sort of agreement on pitch, but it might change from place to place. This was all right when nobody moved around much, but for travelling musicians it started to become a problem — not to mention expensive, since you might need to have a different instrument for each gig you played.

Although standardized pitch wasn't really developed until well into the 18th century, by the time of the Renaissance in the 16th and early 17th centuries some progress had been made toward standardizing musical instruments.

Maybe people's ears hurt from listening to all those loud shawms and trumpets, but by the early 16th century, musicians began to favor the softer-sounding instruments such as the recorder, the lute and the viol. Maybe they were getting a headache.[10]

Aside from turning down the volume, the Renaissance brought another basic shift in musical ideals. Instead of the heterogeneous, or mixed, sound of the Middle Ages, composers and listeners began to favor the blended sound of different sizes of the same instrument. This sound is called *homogeneous,* another fancy term from the Greek *homo,* meaning "the same." (Think of homogenized milk, which is blended together, and you'll get the idea.)

If you wanted a really homogeneous sound, one of the best things to do was to have a whole set or family of instruments by

---

[10] When King Ferdinand of Bavaria came to visit the Duke of Ferrara one day in 1566, he was greeted by a fanfare of cornets and trombones — playing in the next room.

the same maker, made together to assure a better blend. Such a collection of instruments was known as a *chest* — a chest of viols, say, or a chest of recorders — since they actually came packed up in a chest for easier storage. A chest of viols might include two trebles, two tenors and two basses.

An ensemble of the same instruments together came to be called a *consort*, and it became popular in the Renaissance — if you could afford that sort of thing — to have a consort of recorders or a consort of viols playing quiet music while you dined or whatever. If you were very wealthy, you could consort with your consort while a consort played in the background. (You could, I suppose, have a consort of shawms, but that would rather spoil the mood.)

There were actually two types of consort: the "whole" consort, made up of similar instruments, and the "broken" consort, made up of different instruments, such as some recorders and viols together with a lute — whatever worked, as long as the sound wasn't too strident. (Broken consorts are also the ones you accidentally dropped down the stairs.)

English composers of the Elizabethan era wrote a whole slew of music for a special broken consort consisting of flute (or recorder), violin (or treble viol), lute, bass viol, cittern and pandora. This group was often used in the theatre for plays by Shakespeare and others and is often called the Morley consort, after Thomas Morley (1557-1603), the English composer who wrote whole books of music for this type of gang. (Don't confuse the Morley consort with a motley consort, which is something else again.)

As the Renaissance gave way to the Baroque, instruments continued to develop and change, generally becoming more and more standardized and more like the ones we have today. This made it easier for musicians to play together, and eventually led to the development of the modern orchestra. That's all well and good, but I can't help thinking that the loss of variety took some of the fun out of things, now that we don't have nearly as many different instruments to choose from.

Who knows? Maybe some budding Renaissance instrument maker, tinkering away in his workshop, changed the whole course of musical development and was forever traumatized when his parents shouted at him, "Stop making such a rackett!"

C H A P T E R

LET'S SING
MADRIGALS, GUYS

BEFORE THERE WERE Nintendo games, before there were music videos on MuchMusic or MTV to watch, people had to come up with ways to entertain themselves after dinner, or on rainy days when they were stuck indoors.

One of the easiest forms of entertainment was to make music, either by playing instruments or by singing songs, whether solo songs with accompaniment or songs for small groups of singers. (We're talking here, of course, about secular music, as opposed to church music. After all, people had to do *something* when they weren't in church.)

Indeed, as English composer and theorist Thomas Morley explains in his instruction book *A Plaine And Easie Introduction To Practicall Musicke,* published in 1597, the ability to sing was considered an essential part of any decent education and upbringing. Here's the little scenario by which Morley's book explains it:

"Supper being ended, and the Musicke bookes, according to the custome being brought to the table, the mistresse of the house presented mee with a part, earnestly requesting mee to sing. But when, after many excuses, I protested unfainedly that I could not: everie one began to wonder. Yea, some whispered to others, demanding how I was brought up."

So, says Morley, if you can't sing madrigals, you haven't been raised properly. Which is where he comes in. Morley, in other words, uses guilt and his readers' fears of being hopelessly out of touch to increase the sales of his own book: a useful technique, and one that continues to the present day. Maybe I should try it.[1]

Certainly, children growing up in the best households would be taught at least some basic skills in singing and other music making, but even the poorer folk who couldn't afford fancy music instructors would have learned enough about music to join in the singing when the after-dinner entertainments began.

Not everyone, however, believed singing to be the necessary virtue that Morley insists on. Take for instance the Italian writer Giralomo Cardano (1501-1576), who sometimes went by the name Hieronymous Cardanus, who had this to say about singers: "Their morals are depraved, they are gluttons and disreputable purveyors of every kind of vice." Maybe he just wasn't hanging around with the right people.

Moreover, he says, singers act like fools, partly because all of them drink too much. But we shouldn't be too hard on singers, he says. They can't help it. Stupidity is an occupational hazard, "because their musical tones are carried to the brain with force and weaken it." Well, that explains everything.[2]

But Cardano was obviously a bit of a sorehead. Most other people agreed that the ability to sing, even a little bit, was something everybody should have. People who don't know music, writes the English essayist Henry Peacham in his book *The Compleat Gentleman* (1622), are "of such a brutish stupidity that scarce anything else that is good and savoreth of virtue is to be found in them." You tell 'em, Hank.

Needless to say, all this push for solo and ensemble vocal music kept the composers busy churning out material to satisfy a demanding market.

This had begun in the 12th and 13th centuries, when the troubadours and trouveres wandered around continental Europe singing pretty little songs, or chansons. This was a relatively new

[1] Whatever the virtues of Morley's musical education, he certainly wasn't the greatest when it came to spelling and punctuation.
[2] "They also teach," Cardano adds, "but their pedagogy is senseless."

occupation, and everyone was pretty excited about it. "The poetry of the troubadours," says historian Robert Briffault in his little book on the subject, "answered the mood of a feudal society newly awakened to a sense of its native uncouthness." The troubadour tradition had started in France, where they don't like to be considered uncouth. It's bad for the image.

Most these songs had to do with the singer's unrequited love for some other man's wife (or, usually in the case of female troubadours and trouveres, some woman's husband). It was one of the requirements of the job that the object of affection in whatever song they sang had to be married to someone else or otherwise unattainable by virtue of social standing, temperament or other such obstacle (even by virtue of virtue). Anything else and they risked being thrown out of the troubadour's union.

The chief difference between troubadours and trouveres, by the way, is one of geography: troubadours generally covered the southern territory and trouveres covered the north. Presumably the ones from the south would shiver a bit if you brought them north, whereas the northerners might sunburn easily. Other than that, it's pretty hard to tell them apart. (Some grouchy historians think that the trouveres are just copycats, stealing all their best ideas from the troubadours. "The amorous poetry of the north," says Paul Meyer, "is considerably inferior to its southern sister." I don't have an opinion either way myself.[3]

Troubadour songs were generally solo songs (even if two men were in love with the same woman, they didn't customarily sing about it together) with a simple accompaniment by lute or other such easily portable instrument. (They had to be able to pick up and run, just in case hubby came along.)

The accompaniment wasn't usually written down or even strictly codified: whoever was playing the instrumental backup (either another musician or the troubadour himself) would simply

[3] In Germany, these performers were called *minnesingers* – maybe because they were a smaller group.

improvise based on the original tune. Musicologists, who like to use fancy terms to make themselves sound important, call this *heterophony*. The rest of us would probably call it "faking it."

From this tradition developed two parallel genres of music: the solo song with instrumental accompaniment, and the part-song, for two or more voices (it usually came to be four, but sometimes as many as eight).

The terminology of these two basic forms is, to put it mildly, a confusing mess. In Germany, the term *lied* generally refers to a song for solo voice with instrumental accompaniment. But it is also used for a song for two or more voices. In France, the term *chanson* can likewise mean either a solo or polyphonic work, sometimes also called an *air de cour* ("court song"). In Italy, they generally used the term *ballata* for solo works and *frottola* or *madrigal* for polyphonic ones. In England the solo song was often called an *ayre*, while the polyphonic work used the borrowed Italian term *madrigal*. (Though, just to be as confusing as everywhere else, they sometimes called the polyphonic ones ayres, too).[4]

Other terms you might come across in a more detailed study of this type of music (i.e. in a book more serious than this one) include *caccia, virelai, canzona, balletto, villancico* and *strambotto*, just to name a few.[5]

The 14th-century Italian madrigal was very popular in its day, but you don't hear much about it anymore, except among people who really like that sort of thing.[6]

Nowadays when people use the term madrigal, they usually mean those songs for four or more parts written in the

[4] These songs became particularly popular among the English royalty and nobility. They like putting on ayres.

[5] I could at this point mention the *capitolo,* the *rondeau* or the *canzonet,* but why complicate things?

[6] Music lovers who like to impress their friends will refer to 14th-century Italy as the *trecento* period (meaning the 1300s). They'll go on an on about the loveliness and craft of *trecento* music. (For hours, if you let them.) For some reason, you never hear them talk about the 15th century as *quadracento* or the 16th century as *quinquecento*. Funny how that happens.

16th and early 17th centuries, chiefly in Italy or England (the Italian ones in Italian and the English ones in English, usually, just to keep everything orderly). Because they have several different voice parts, they are sometimes called "part songs," which seems logical. In England they were sometimes called "prick songs," but not for the reason you might expect: it only meant they were actually written down (by the pricking of pen on paper, if you must know).

By the 16th century the traditions of the solo song and the part song were well established. Anybody who was anybody wrote them, from Lassus to Sermisy to Josquin. The French composer Jannequin was famous for writing chansons in which the singers imitate nifty sound effects of birds chirping or cannons firing or whatever. (It took a few more centuries for Tchaikovsky to come along and use real cannons, in his *1812 Overture.* Jannequin probably would have used real cannons, too, if he'd had the budget.)

Musicologists, who like things to be organized, often divide songs into two categories, depending on the way the music fits the text. If it uses the same music for each verse (the way a church hymn does, for instance), they call it *strophic,* which means exactly that but sounds more impressive. If the music changes for each verse, musicologists use the term "through-composed." Or, if they really want to sound impressive, they switch to German and dazzle you with *durchkomponiert.* In general, solo songs tend to be strophic, while part songs tend to be *durchkomponiert,* but that's just a general rule. I wouldn't bet next week's pay on it or anything.

Sometimes it was difficult to tell the solo song and the part song apart: composers would write a melody with words on top and then fill in underneath with a few other parts that could be sung, if you had singers, or played as accompaniment on the lute or by other instruments or with whatever keyboard you happened to have lying around.

England developed an especially strong tradition in both areas, often overlapping. Composers such as Byrd, Morley, Thomas Weelkes, Orlando Gibbons and a whole bunch of others wrote more songs and madrigals than you can shake a stick at. You'd think they had nothing better to do. (Maybe they didn't.)

Among the most famous of the English composers of this period was John Dowland (1562-1626). He spent his early career traipsing around the Continent, in Paris, parts of Germany and Denmark, before returning to London and becoming court composer to James I. (He probably did a little spying on the side and somewhere along the way, historians point out, he lost his Catholicism. Maybe it wasn't lost, just misplaced.)[7]

Dowland was a terrific lute player, or lutenist, and his specialty in writing lute songs was the mournful, tearful lament. Other composers wrote some pretty soppy stuff, too (let's not forget John Benet's *Weep, O Mine Eyes* or Thomas Campian's rousing *Break Now My Heart And Die*), but nobody beats Dowland for sheer consistency. At times, he can be downright depressing.

You can tell just by looking at all the Dowland song titles that mention crying: *Flow My Teares, Go Christall Teares, Weepe You No More, I Saw My Lady Weepe* (not to mention the watery *Dowland's Adew*). Maybe after writing them he felt better, but listening to them can be a real downer.

Madrigals and other songs continued in England into the 17th century, although after that composers had pretty much lost interest. Maybe they were all cried out.[8]

After the 16th century the Italians got sidetracked into writing operas, so their solo songs developed into full-blown arias, while the Germans and Austrians began concentrating on

---

[7] That 18th-century English historian and windbag Dr. Charles Burney, in *A General History Of Music*, says Dowland is over-rated as a composer. But then, Burney is over-rated as a historian, so why should we care what he thinks?

[8] An interest in part songs resurfaced in early 20th-century North America with the introduction of barbershop and doo-wop harmony. But that's a different story.

lieder in preparation for the work of such 19th-century composers as Franz Schubert, Robert Schumann and Hugo Wolf.

As the Renaissance era evolved into the Baroque, the stage was now set — literally — for composers to move on to other areas. Or arias.

ARIAS OF INFLUENCE

READERS INTERESTED IN a complete history of the development of opera from the 17th century to the present are not going to find it here.

I would be happy, however, to suggest other reading material. You might start with my previous book *When The Fat Lady Sings: Opera History As It Ought To Be Taught* (Sound And Vision, 1990). If you're really in a hurry, try chapter 9, *A Ridiculously Short History Of Opera*, from my book *Bach, Beethoven, And The Boys* (Sound And Vision, 1986). (Well, of *course* I'm going to recommend my own books first: a fellow's got to eat, you know.)[1]

So, having covered this ground at some length already, I'm not about to do it again. And that's all there is to it.

But, just for fun, let's look for a moment at the development of one particular aspect of opera history, namely the *aria*.

Arias in opera were nothing new, of course, having already been found in the motets, cantatas and oratorios of the early 17th centuries and even before.

In whatever genre, the aria is pretty much the same thing: a song for solo voice with accompaniment. Or sometimes two voices, in which case it's a duet aria. In opera, usually a love duet. (Pretty much the whole second act of Wagner's *Tristan und Isolde* is a love duet. And boy does it get tiresome.)

---

[1] If you really insist on looking somewhere else, there's a book by that fellow Grout that should clear up any of the little details.

A big, full-blown aria is generally introduced by a shorter movement called a *recitative,* in which the singer recites the text in a sort of conversational singing style. Recitatives (or "recits," if you want to speak the lingo) are useful for getting a lot of information across quickly and for keeping the plot moving, since it pretty much grinds to a halt each time an aria comes along.

The first use of the term aria in the history of opera, Grout tells us (and he should know), is found in *La catena d'Adone,* "The Chain Of Adonis," composed by Domenico Mazzocchi (1592-1665) and performed in Rome in 1626.[2]

The earliest arias were often strophic but composers grew tired of that and pretty soon they were generally through-composed — which in German, you'll remember, is *durchkomponiert.*[3]

The real problems began when these arias started becoming longer and more elaborate, as a way for the composer and singer to show off how talented they were (or, in some cases, only how talented they *thought* they were). It's hard to know whom to blame here: the singers for wanting flashier and flashier arias to sing, or the composers for indulging the singers by writing them.

The chief culprit in all of this, of course, is the *da capo* aria, a term that comes from the Italian meaning "to the head."[4]

The *da capo* aria comes in three parts, or really two parts with a repeat: you sing the first section, you sing a second section that contrasts the first, and then you repeat the first section, this time with lots of ornaments and nifty special effects.

---

[2] Mazzocchi meant well, but he hadn't quite figured it out: he called nearly everything an aria, whether it was a solo song, a duet or even the chorus stuff. Well, it was a start.

[3] My knowledge of German is a little patchy, so I can't be certain whether *durchkomponiert* is in any way related to *durchfall,* the German word for diarrhea. It might be.

[4] Remember what Giralomo Cardano said about singers in the previous chapter? He said the musical tones "are carried to the brain with force and weaken it." Maybe that's what *da capo* really means

This is known as *ternary,* or ABA form, and Baroque opera lovers thought it was just the greatest thing since sliced bread.

Most scholars generally credit the composer Alessandro Scarlatti (1660-1725) with creating the *da capo* aria, on the theory that they have to blame *someone.* He first thought of it in his opera *Teodora,* in 1693. After that, there was no turning back.

It didn't take very long for the *da capo* aria to become the chief vehicle (some might say chief weapon) of composers from the 17th and 18th centuries, and even into the 19th, whether they were writing opera, oratorio or any other big musical production.

In opera more than anywhere else, this emphasis on arias — and on the big egos of the performers who sang them — reduced the chorus to a much smaller and less important role. (The composer and theorist Giovanni Andrea Bontempi, writing in 1662, says choruses should only be used in oratorios, and that's that.)

This, of course, is one of the chief differences between opera and oratorio, where the use of the chorus is more evenly balanced with that of solo arias and duets. Handel stopped writing operas late in his career and turned instead to writing oratorios. Maybe he just got tired of having to deal with all those arrogant, temperamental opera singers. (Especially the *castrati,* those male singers who had "lost their marbles," as it were, to preserve their high notes.)[5]

Handel's relationships with his singers were often fiery, to say the least. Shortly after hiring the celebrated Italian castrato Senesino in 1720, Handel began referring to him as "a damned fool." After that they were barely civil to one another. Handel should have known what he was in for: earlier that year Senesino had been fired from the Dresden opera company for refusing to sing an aria in *Flavio Crispo,* by Johann David Heinichen. He just tore up the music and stomped off the stage.

[5] Bontempi was a castrato, which may account for his bad temper. He felt he was missing something.

Not all of Handel's singers were castrati, of course. There were the rival sopranos Faustina and Cuzzoni, and in 1724 Handel took the unusual step (unusual for 1724, anyway) of hiring an Italian tenor, Francesco Borosini, who performed in Handel's opera *Tamerlano*.[6]

Singers love the *da capo* aria, of course, because it guarantees them an encore and because the built-in repeat gives them a chance to really show off. Sometimes, the repeat is so full of extra runs, trills and other fancy doodads that you'd hardly recognize that it's supposed to be the same music. (The Italians call this elaborate type of singing *coloratura*, or "colored," because the long whole notes are filled in, or colored in, by a lot of faster little notes.)[7]

As the *da capo* aria continued to develop, the practice of ornamentation became more and more extreme. In fact, it had started to get out of hand. (Pietro Francesco Tosi, writing in 1723, says that for a singer's final cadenza, "The throat is set a-going like a weathercock in a whirlwind, and the orchestra yawns.")

Gioacchino Rossini (1792-1868) was one composer who got so tired of singers destroying his music by over-elaborating on it that he started writing out the ornaments he wanted, beginning in 1815 with his opera *Elisabetta, regina d'Inghilterra*, ("Elizabeth, Queen of England"). This worked for a while, as long as Rossini was around to police things. But as soon as his back was turned, those singers would start up again. Rossini, who as a child had been apprenticed to a blacksmith, learned to forge on regardless.

Richard Wagner (1813-1883) dealt with this problem another way: after *Lohengrin* (he finished it in 1848 but couldn't convince anybody to perform it until 1850), he simply got rid of recits and arias altogether, and wrote his operas in a more or

---

[6] The fact that Borosini wasn't a castrato prompted one wag to remark that "this gentleman was never cut out for a singer."

[7] Nowadays performers sometimes call all the black notes "flyshit," but generally not in polite company.

less continuous fashion. He called this *unendliche Melodie,* or "endless melody," because it goes on forever.

Despite his best efforts, Wagner did manage to write some good tunes, even nice hummable ones. It would probably bother him to no end to realize that a chorus from Act III of *Lohengrin* has become vastly popular as *Here Comes The Bride*.

Wagner, by the way, didn't call his works operas, he called them "music dramas." But it amounts to the same thing. Wagner liked to think he was composing *Zukunftsmusik,* or "the music of the future." He wasn't.[8]

Other composers since Wagner — Verdi, Puccini and Richard Strauss, just to name a few — justifiably ignored his example and continued writing recits and arias just as before, though the *da capo* aria had already begun to lose favor long before Wagner stepped in and completely quashed it.

I suppose we should thank him for that, but considering the alternative he gave us, I'm not so sure.

[8] In the last decade of his life, Wagner and his wife Cosima (Liszt's daughter and Hans von Bülow's ex) moved into a house he named *Wahnfried,* which is German for "peace from madness." Even *he* needed a place to get away from his own operas.

CHAPTER

12

SHALL WE DANCE?

DANCING AND MUSIC have existed together pretty much from the start. It's a bit of a chicken-and-egg question as to which came first, dancing or music.[1]

The earliest dances were likely some sort of fertility rites, and were the human equivalent of animal mating dances.[2] Dancing also came to be associated with other major events in the life cycle, including death — the so-called *danse macabre*.[3]

In the Middle Ages, dancing became more formalized. Bureaucracy had started to take over. Doesn't it always?

Different types of dances were developed, each with its own style of rhythm and movement. The form of these dances began to influence both music and literature. (It's no coincidence that we speak of poetry having "feet.")

In the Renaissance, dances became separated into two general categories: the stiff, formal, dignified dancing of the aristocracy and upper classes, and the livelier, more entertaining dances of the peasants and lower classes, which were generally much more fun.[4]

---

[1] If dancing came first, music probably wasn't very far behind: people look awfully silly dancing around when there's no music in the background.

[2] The pavane, a popular dance of the 16th century, comes from the Italian term *pavoggionare*, which means to "strut like a peacock."

[3] An edict by the ninth-century Pope Leo IV banned dancing at gravesides. It gave him the willies.

[4] The *tarantella*, a frantic Italian dance, is named after the tarantula spider, supposedly because the tarantula's poison made you move in a frenzied dance. Dancing fast enough was also supposed to cure you. It probably couldn't hurt.

Queen Elizabeth I of England scandalized her court by dancing a *volta*, a particularly vigorous dance with a lot of leaps and turns. People thought it wasn't dignified. But that's what she liked about being queen: she could do whatever she wanted.[5]

Among the earliest dance forms were the *branle* or *bransle*, and the *estampie* or *estampida*, which got its name because it involved stamping on the ground. Another is the *basse danse*, which means "low dance." Scholars are still arguing over whether that means low because it came from the peasants or low because you dance it without lifting your feet very high. If they ever make up their minds, I'll let you know.

The *basse danse* is a slowish dance in duple (as opposed to triple) time. It was later replaced by the *pavane*, a similarly slow and stately dance. *Pavanes* were danced by the aristocrats. They thought it made them look important.

One of the most famous treatises on early dance is *Orchesographie*, written by Jehan Tabourot and published in 1588. (He wrote it under the pen name Thoinot Arbeau, probably because he was a priest and the church didn't approve of dancing.) Like many theoretical treatises of that time, it's written in the form of a dialogue between the teacher, Arbeau, and his particularly dim-witted pupil, Capriol.[6]

"Let the noble gentleman dance it with sword and beret," Arbeau says, describing the *pavane*. "The ladies show a modest demeanor, lower their eyes and only from time to time glance up at the audience with maidenly coyness."[7]

The *pavane* was often followed by another popular dance of the time, the *galliard*. (The name may come from *galleus*, a

---

[5] Dancing was sometimes a hazardous occupation: at a dance before the 15th-century king Charles VI of France, the costumes of some of the dancers accidentally caught fire from a torch. In the confusion, two members of the audience were burned to death. The king, needless to say, was upset.

[6] Tabourot is having a little joke here: *capriol* means "somersault."

[7] They had to glance up from time to time just to watch out for the swords.

type of French apple, but the scholars are still arguing over that one, too.) The *galliard* was a much livelier dance with a lot of high stepping (Arbeau says you should lift your leg as if you're about to kick someone). Because it involved a pattern of five steps, it was sometimes known in Italian as *cinque passi* and in French as *cinque pas*. (The English, never very good at translating from other languages, called it "sink-a-pace").[8]

As often happens, music meant for dancing also worked its way into other performing situations, combining musical influences from a variety of countries. Renaissance composers often wrote dance-like music, such as sets of pavanes and galliards, that may have been meant only for listening to, not dancing. In the Renaissance and Baroque, dance pieces were grouped together into suites, which formed the basis for the sonata and later the symphony.

These instrumental suites might include such dances as the French *courante*, the German *allemande*, the Spanish *sarabande* or the Italian *saltarello*. (The *bourée*, a French dance, gets its name from the word for flapping wings.)

Early Baroque dancing, or ballet (from the Latin word *ballare*, meaning "to dance"), was generally not treated as a separate art form, but was usually incorporated as part of some larger performance — first in allegorical spectacles and later as part of an opera.

The aristocrats loved big, fancy productions because it gave them a chance to dress up in funny costumes. When Ferdinand III of Austria married the Spanish princess Maria Anna in Vienna in 1631, for instance, there was a big ballet production in which the Archduchess Claudia dressed up as the moon, with other ladies of the court dressing up as the planets. They had a grand old time.

A little later, in 1667, when Leopold I married another Spanish princess, Margarita, there was a special performance of

---

[8] Michael Praetorius, the 16th-century German music theorist, was no better. In his encyclopedia *Syntagma Musicum* he calls it a *gagliard*.

Cesti's *opera Il pomo d'oro* ("The Golden Apple"), with lots of dancing beforehand. The opera libretto is based on the famous Greek myth about Paris giving a golden apple to Venus, the goddess of love, who then helped him win the heart of Helen of Troy, thereby starting the Trojan War.[9]

Cesti, no fool when it came to sucking up to his royal patron, altered the plot for this occasion, having the actor playing Paris give the golden apple to Margarita instead.[10]

It was in the 17th century that French ballet started to become an important force in its own right. But still it was regarded more as an entertainment than an art form. Along about 1645, there was a performance for the future King Louis XIV of France of *La finta pazza*, a ballet by the Venetian composer Francesco Sacrati. In addition to the costumed dancers, the orchestra dressed up in animal skins and there were clowns doing tricks and pratfalls. Louis thought it was marvelous — of course, he was about six years old at the time.

When Louis XIV got married in 1660 (to yet another Spanish princess, Maria Theresa), there was a special performance of Cavalli's opera *Serse*, for which a young Italian musician named Giovanni Battista Lulli wrote special ballet music. (Writing music for the king's wedding was a step up for Lulli, who'd started out in the kitchen as a busboy.)

The king was impressed by Lulli, who soon changed his name to the French version, Jean-Baptiste Lully. He joined the court orchestra, Les 24 violins du Roi ("The 24 violins of the King"), and soon became its leader. Lully got himself appointed court composer and, after a fight with the 24 violins, formed another group, *Les 16 petits violons*, or "The 16 little violins."[11]

In addition to his talents as a composer and player, Lully was by all accounts an accomplished dancer who often performed in his own ballets. Sometimes the king joined in, too, just to

---

[9] Homer wrote a word or two on the subject, you'll remember.

[10] It sheer diplomacy: Margarita, we are told, was "ugly as a mole."

[11] I don't think the violins were actually little, I think they were the regular size. Maybe the players were little.

show he was a good sport. (But usually he played the part of a king or a god, just to show that he was still in charge.)

Under Lully, ballet became an important part of French theatre, and was almost always included in any performance of opera, a tradition that lasted well into the 19th century.[12]

Lully's influence on French music came to a sudden end in 1687, after he bashed his toe with a big staff, which in those days was pounded on the floor to beat time for the music. Lully's stubbed toe developed gangrene, which led to blood poisoning and eventually his death. I suppose it's appropriate, if ironic, that the composer who first popularized ballet should die of a foot injury.

Important ballet composers after Lully include Rameau and Gluck, whose ballet version of *Don Juan* was performed in 1761. The young Mozart wrote one ballet, *Les Petits Riens*, in 1778, hoping it would get him some more work. It didn't. (Maybe it was the title: calling it "The Little Nothings" surely doesn't inspire confidence.)

Beethoven, being too busy revolutionizing the symphonic form, found time to write only one ballet, *The Creatures of Prometheus*, in 1800 or so.

Even Wagner had to swallow his pride and bow to the French predilection for the dance, inserting a specially composed ballet into his opera *Tannhäuser* for a performance in Paris in 1860. But Wagner blew it: not wanting to tamper much with his opera, he put the ballet near the very beginning. This enraged the Parisian high-society set, who liked to arrive at the opera house fashionably late, in time for a ballet in the second act. The ensuing riots closed the production after only three performances.

Ballet really came into its own in the 19th century, with works such as Adolphe Adam's *Giselle* (1841) and *Coppelia*, by Leo Delibes (1870), paving the way for ballets of Tchaikovsky, who came later.

---

[12] It became what you might call a shoo-in.

Pyotr Illyich Tchaikovsky (1840-93) wrote an early version of *Swan Lake* in 1871 to amuse the children of his sister Alexandra Davidov. He expanded it for a professional performance in Moscow in 1877. About one-third of the music was omitted from this first performance: the performers said it was too hard to dance to.[13]

Tchaikovsky followed up with *Sleeping Beauty* in 1890 and *The Nutcracker* in 1892. (For *The Dance of the Sugar Plum Fairy* in *The Nutcracker,* Tchaikovsky introduced the first use of a new instrument called the *celesta,* a kind of piano that sounds like bells. He'd heard it in Paris the year before and decided he just had to have one.)

None of Tchaikovsky's ballets was particularly well received at its premiere performance, but nowadays they're big hits with ballet lovers.[14]

Such was the appetite for ballet in the 19th and early 20th centuries that even works not specifically written as dance music were arranged for ballet performances. Opera music by Rossini, Donizetti and Verdi, for instance, has been adapted for ballet. The popular one-act ballet *Les Sylphides* is based on piano music by Frederic Chopin.[15]

One of the most important figures in 20th-century ballet is the impresario Sergei Diaghilev, who founded *Les Ballets Russes,* or The Russian Ballet, in Paris in 1909. He brought together such important artists as choreographer Michel Fokine, dancers Vaslav Nijinsky and Anna Pavlova, and composers Igor Stravinsky and Sergei Prokofiev. Add Pablo Picasso to do some set designs and you've got one heck of a company.

Quite aside from assembling such an array of talent, Diaghilev's company made two other important contributions

---

[13] Funny, nobody seems to have that trouble now.

[14] For reasons I've never fully understood, ballet lovers are called *balletomanes.* But you never hear of *symphonomanes* or *concertomanes* or *motetomanes.* I wonder why?

[15] It was originally called *Chopiniana,* which didn't seem to catch on.

to the development of ballet. It replaced the traditional three-act ballet with three shorter one-act works — an innovation welcomed by audiences with short attention spans — and encouraged composers to adapt music not originally written for dancing. (It was Folkine who had thought of arranging Chopin, but Diaghilev who came up with the brainstorm of changing the name from *Chopiniana*. That's teamwork for you.)

Among Stravinsky's most important ballets for Diaghilev are *L'Oiseau de Feu* ("The Firebird") in 1910 and *Petrouchka* in 1911.[16]

But Stravinsky's most important ballet, and one of his most important works overall, is *Le Sacre du Printemps* ("The Rite of Spring"). The first performance, on May 29, 1913 in Paris, caused quite a sensation. The strange music, with its oddly pulsing rhythms, and the storyline about pagans sacrificing a young woman to the God of Spring, got the audience very upset. People were rioting in their seats, demanding their money back and falling all over each other in a rush to leave the theatre. To make matters worse, Nijinsky made a very rude gesture to the audience, which even the Parisians found offensive.

Nijinsky had a hard time with *Le Sacre* all around. At the rehearsals, Stravinsky had to teach him the rhythms by banging them out on an old tin tray.[17]

After *Le Sacre*, most of the other Diaghilev ballets seem tame by comparison, even the other pagan one, Prokofiev's *Scythian Suite*. (Prokofiev had re-arranged his own music, taking it from his unfinished opera *Ala And Lolly*, written in 1914. Like Bach, he didn't like to see good music go to waste.) Prokofiev later wrote ballet versions of *Romeo And Juliet* and of *Cinderella*, just to keep in practice.

---

[16] Stravinksy scored *The Firebird* for an orchestra including three harps, thinking you can never have too many harps. Yes you can.

[17] Many years later, Stravinsky wrote a polka for the Ringling Brothers circus. It was choreographed by George Balanchine and performed by 50 elephants. They were probably easier to teach.

Maurice Ravel wrote two operas: *Daphnis et Chloe* for Diaghilev in 1912 and *Bolero* in 1928 for the dancer Ida Rubenstein. Ravel once described *Bolero* as "fifteen minutes of orchestra without music." That about sums it up.

Today a dance performance encompasses much more than just ballet. It may include everything from jazz or acrobatic and even animalistic movements to moves inspired by street fighting and break dancing. Lully may be turning over in his grave. Gracefully, of course.

CHAPTER

13

CONCERTED EFFORTS

I T WOULD BE A LOT easier to talk about sonatas, concertos and other similar musical forms (trios, quartets and that sort of thing) if the terminology weren't so darn confusing.

These days there's a general sort of agreement, but only if nobody decides to get too picky. (And you know those musicologists: they love to be picky.)

The *sonata* usually has four movements: a fast opening movement, a slow movement, a graceful, waltz-like minuet movement and another fast movement to finish it off. (In his music, Beethoven replaced the minuet favored by Haydn and Mozart with a *scherzo*, which is a sort of minuet pumped up on steroids.)

The sonata is a showoff piece, generally (but not always) for one solo instrument — maybe a violin, a flute, a clarinet or whatever — with accompaniment usually provided by a keyboard instrument such as a piano. (Before the piano it might have been a harpsichord, but that's another chapter.)

That's OK unless it's a piano sonata, in which case there's only one piano, doing both the showing off and the accompaniment (which in a way is *really* showing off). But a sonata for two pianos doesn't mean that one of them is the soloist and the other is the accompanist, it's really more of a duet for two pianos. Got that? It gets worse.

The *concerto* is a bigger, flashier showoff piece for solo instrument or instruments (violin, piano, flute, bassoon, whatever) with orchestra. It's often longer than a sonata even though it usually has only three movements, fast-slow-fast, with minuet or scherzo. The first movement of a concerto often includes an improvised section near the end called a *cadenza*, which gives the soloist a chance to go nuts and really show off. (The orchestra at this point is usually holding one long note or chord, or wisely just shuts up and stays out of the way until the soloist has run out of things to say.)

A cadenza can be impressive, but only if the person improvising it has some sense of the appropriate style. If not, it can sound like an awful mess. Beethoven must have grown tired of hearing second-rate players massacre his concertos with their cadenzas (he could still hear at this point), so for his *Piano Concerto Op. 73* (the "Emperor" Concerto) he wrote out a complete cadenza, just to be on the safe side. Other composers since Beethoven have done this, too.[1]

Sometimes, composers will write a shorter sonata or concerto in only one movement. This is often called a *sonatina* or *concertina,* meaning "little sonata" or "little concerto."

That's how the terminology generally works today, although some modern composers have tried to confuse us by writing what they called a "Concerto for Orchestra," which seems like a contradiction in terms. Hindemith did this in 1925 and Bartok did the same thing in 1943.[2]

When they weren't writing sonatas, concertos or symphonies (which we'll get to later), composers spent a great deal of time writing what is loosely termed *chamber music.* The term is vague, but is now generally used to refer to music written for a small ensemble of instruments (one instrument to a part, as opposed to a whole orchestra), in which each instrument has a more or less equal role to play.[3]

---

[1] It doesn't always work. Performers still ignore the written cadenzas and make up their own. You can't win.

[2] Bartok's piece is especially confusing: it has five movements.

[3] For this reason some people don't consider the sonata as chamber music, since the soloist is usually more important than the accompaniment. But I say that's just splitting hairs. And besides, how else are you going to classify it?

On the whole, the terminology in chamber music is a little less confusing, since it tends to be more sensible. A work for flute, oboe and bassoon, say, is generally just called a trio for flute, oboe and bassoon. What could be simpler? Trios have three instruments, quartets have four, quintets have five and so on up to the nonet, for nine instruments.[4]

The string quartet — which is really a sort of sonata for four stringed instruments — became one of the favorite genres of composers from about Haydn onwards, including Mozart, Beethoven, Dvorak and the rest of those guys. Haydn is sometimes called "the father of the string quartet," having written about 80 of them, give or take. But it hardly seems fair to blame him for all of the others, too.

The opening *allegro,* or fast movement, of many of these genres — sonatas, concertos, a lot of chamber music — most often follows a pattern called *sonata form,* or *sonata allegro form,* or *first movement form.* You could spend your whole career studying the development and treatment of sonata form at the hands of innumerable composers from the Classic period onwards. Feel free, if you want to.

The only real confusion in chamber music — in terminology, at least — comes with an ensemble of strings accompanying another instrument with generally a more important role. So although a string quartet means a work for four strings (two violins, viola and cello), a clarinet quartet is not a piece for four clarinets, it's usually a piece for one clarinet with three strings (violin, viola, cello) as backup. If you really wanted to write a piece for four clarinets (God knows why, but say you did), you'd have to be more specific and call it a quartet for four clarinets.

Sometimes composers just added another instrument to a string quartet, making a quintet. It's as if a string quartet were

---

[4] After that, composers generally stop counting, and so should we. A piece for 13 instruments, I suppose, would be called a *triskaidektet,* but I've never heard of one.

practising and some other instrumentalist just dropped by and decided to sit in.[5]

So much for the accepted terminology of today. Delve any further back into the history of music and you're only asking for trouble.

The term sonata, for example, comes from the Latin *sonare* or the Italian *suonare*, the verb meaning "to sound." Originally, sonata was used for any sort of piece that was "sounded." In other words, just about any composition could be (and was) called a sonata. You can trace the term back to at least the 12th century, if not earlier, and it crops up all the time in the 15th and 16th.

Italian and other European composers in the 16th and early 17th centuries wrote works called the *ricercare* or the *canzona*, which are polyphonic, often imitative pieces rather like motets or chansons or madrigals for instruments instead of voices. They were sometimes called *canzone da sonar*, or "chansons for sounding," from which developed the term sonata. These were still ensemble pieces, not for solo instrument and accompaniment. They were often in several contrasting sections or movements, not unlike dance suites.

In the Baroque period, the sonata came to be divided into two main categories, the *sonata da chiesa* and the *sonata da camera*, or the "church" sonata and the "chamber" sonata. At first this distinction was purely arbitrary, referring only to the place where the music might be performed, either at church or at home.

But later, chiefly under the influence of the Italian violinist and composer Archangelo Corelli (1653-1713), the *sonata da chiesa* became a work in four movements (slow-fast-slow-fast), whereas the *sonata da camera* became a suite with an introduction followed by three or four little dances. (Even then, this was

---

[5] Despite this logic, however, Haydn's *Razor Quartet* (Op. 55, No. 2 in F minor) is not a work for string quartet and solo razor. Razors are just too hard to tune, and you'd never hear one over the sound of all those violins.

merely a ruse. The "church" sonata often had dance movements that just weren't labelled that way, on the theory that
what people don't know won't hurt them: the church takes a
dim view of dancing.)

But the terminology got even more confusing in the Baroque,
since the term sonata was also used for almost any sort of
chamber work for instruments. Or even one instrument, such
as Bach's sonatas for solo violin and solo cello.

A different kettle of fish entirely is the Baroque *trio sonata*,
which despite what its name suggests actually requires four
players: there are two upper parts, more or less equal, providing
a kind of melodic dialogue; a cello or *viola da gamba* playing the
bass line; and a harpsichord or some other keyboard instrument (sometimes a lute) filling in the harmony. Baroque
composers including Bach, Handel, Purcell, Corelli and Vivaldi
wrote altogether hundreds of trio sonatas. It kept them out of
trouble.[6]

The concerto, meanwhile, was also going through some
changes of its own. Although we now use it to describe
instrumental music, the term concerto was originally used for
vocal or choral works with instrumental accompaniment. The
Gabrielis — Andrea and his nephew — Giovanni wrote choral
concertos in Venice in the late 16th century.

Scholars are divided, by the way, over the origin of the
term concerto. Some say it comes from the Latin *concertare*,
meaning "to fight" or "to quarrel," and from the related word
concertator, meaning "rival." Other scholars, with a sunnier
disposition, say the term comes from the Latin *conserere*, meaning "to join together, to unite."

So either a concerto is a sort of rivalry contest in which the
soloist(s) and orchestra fight it out in a contest of musical skill,
or the two groups join together co-operatively to create music.
It's a bit like trying to decide whether a glass is half-empty or

---

[6] Many historians consider the *sonata da chiesa* and the *sonata da camera*
as variants of the *trio sonata*. I say let them.

half-full: it depends on how you look at it.[7]

In the later Renaissance and early Baroque, the term concerto came to describe works for contrasting "choirs" of instruments instead of voices. From this came the genre called the *concerto grosso*, or "big concerto," a Baroque forerunner of the later symphony. The *concerto grosso* includes several movements and sets up a contrast between a small group of solo instruments and the larger full orchestra. Music that pits one instrument, or group of instruments, against another is said to be in *concertato* style.

The small group is called the *principale*, or sometimes the *concertino*.[8] The larger group is called the *tutti* (from the Italian meaning "all" or "everybody") or sometimes the *ripieno* (from the Italian meaning "replenished"). The *ripieno* orchestra, in other words, is the musical equivalent of cavalry reinforcements, sent to rescue the smaller group when it was running out of energy.

The *concerto grosso* became very popular with Baroque composers: Corelli wrote quite a few, and Handel wrote a set of them in his Opus 6. Bach's *Brandenburg Concertos* are actually *concerti grossi* (to use the highfalutin Italian form of the plural). And Vivaldi, being Vivaldi, wrote them like they were going out of style (which by his time they were).[9]

The Classical period — the heyday of Haydn, Mozart, Beethoven and their buddies — saw the gradual development of the sonata and concerto forms I described at the beginning of the chapter. If you don't remember, you'd better go back and read it again. And take notes if you have to.

---

[7] English has similar ambiguities: the word "cleave" can mean "to split apart" or "to cling together."

[8] Don't confuse this with the *concertino* meaning "little concerto." We'll never get out of this mess if you do.

[9] Maybe to save time, Vivaldi wrote his with only three movements, the same fast-slow-fast of the solo concerto.

KEYBOARD INPUT

THE MODERN PIANO IS more properly called the *pianoforte*, from the Italian words meaning "soft-loud." It was preceded by the *fortepiano*, or "loud-soft."[1]

The *pianoforte*, or just plain piano, is now one of the most important instruments we have, useful both as a solo instrument (for it can provide both its own melody and accompaniment) and as a sometimes begrudging supporter of the musical expression of other instruments of all shapes and sizes.

The piano and its forebears are keyboard instruments, so called because they have a horizontal row of keys by which the sound is generated. (Actually two rows, with the smaller narrow keys set back slightly from the larger wide ones. Nowadays the wide ones are white and the narrow ones are black, but until the 18th century or so the color scheme was the other way around. I have no idea why.)

Composers and instrument builders have been coming up with all sorts of elaborate ways to make keyboards work for the last couple of thousand years. Most of them now think they've finally got it right. Maybe they have.

The organ, the oldest of the keyboard instruments, is slightly different from the rest because its sound is made by causing air to blow through a series of pipes. It's a sort of wind instrument operated by a keyboard. All of the others in the family are really stringed instruments operated by keyboards.

---

[1] To the best of my knowledge, there was never any such instrument as the *pianopiano* ("soft - soft") or the *forteforte* ("loud - loud"). You'd think someone might have thought of it, but no one ever has.

Apart from the ancient Greek and Roman instrument called the *hydraulus* (check your notes from Chapter 9), the earliest organs in Western music show up around the eighth century or so.

The first organs were big, cumbersome and probably painful to play: they had very few keys and you had to bash down on them with your fist to make the sound come out. Obviously, something had to be done.

A little later came two smaller types of organs: the small *portative* (or portable) organ and the slightly larger *positive* (or positioned) organ. The *portative* was a bit like the present-day accordion: you slung it around your neck and operated a little set of bellows with one hand while playing on the keyboard with the other. It was useful for church processions and that sort of thing. (The 14th-century composer Francesco Landini was apparently a real whiz at the *portative*, a regular Spike Jones of his day.)

The *positive* was actually portable, too, but only if you had four or five hefty people to do the lifting, so it wasn't the sort of instrument you wanted for a lengthy processional. It tended to be placed on top of a table somewhere and left there until somebody got really ambitious and decided to dust.

In the Baroque period, the organ grew larger and became a built-in feature in most churches. Often they would have two or three keyboards played by hand (and called manuals) and another keyboard for the feet, called pedals. As the Baroque progressed, organs (and organ music) grew increasingly more elaborate and complex.[2]

Buxtehude, Frescobaldi, Bach, Handel and other composers of the Baroque wrote vast amounts of music for the organ, from the simplest chorales and hymn tunes to the most com-

---

[2] It occurs to me that one might draw an amusing parallel between the church organ and the modern-day automatic dishwasher, which similarly went from a small countertop model a few decades ago to the impressive built-in under-the-counter devices of today. I'll leave it with you to work out the details.

plex toccatas and fugues.[3]

Later Classic and Romantic composers, especially in France, wrote impressive organ works. The rest of the time, the organ was a useful instrument for drowning out the singing of clergy and congregation during the hymns.

The other keyboard instruments produce their sound by means of strings, which are either plucked, struck or sometimes rubbed. Instrument makers were willing to try just about anything until they found whatever worked.

The chief types of keyboard instruments before the piano include the clavichord, the spinet, the virginal and the harpsichord.[4] Each of these instruments can be referred to by the generic term *clavier*, from the French term for keyboard. (In Germany it's *Klavier*, which means the same but somehow looks more German.)

One of the very earliest claviers or keyboard instruments seems to be one called the *echiquier*, which started showing up in the 14th century, and may be French or English, depending on your point of view. In 1360, King Edward III of England gave one to King John II of France, who was known as John the Good, to make amends for having thrown him in jail. (Actually, he was imprisoned in Savoy palace, which hardly qualifies as a jail. Later, Edward let him visit Windsor Castle, where they went hunting together.) It was nothing personal: France and England were fighting The Hundred Years War and John was taken prisoner at the battle of Portiers.

It may surprise you to learn that The Hundred Years War lasted from 1337 to 1453, making it actually 116 years long. It started when John the Good's father, Philip VI, took control of

---

[3] The toccata is a showoff piece for keyboard instruments, derived from the Italian term *toccare,* meaning "touch." You have to be a little touched to play some of them. A fugue is even more complicated — almost as difficult to explain as it is to play. The name comes from the Latin *fuga,* meaning "flight" or "escape." A useful piece of advice in some cases.

[4] I'd just as soon not mention the pantaleon or the regal, if it's all the same to you.

the Duchy of Guyenne, which Edward III felt he was entitled to. From there it just got even more complicated. (John and Edward were somewhat related, being distant cousins by marriage.)[5]

In 1387, King John of Aragon wrote a polite letter to Philip the Bold, Duke of Burgundy, asking if he might borrow Philip's *echiquier*, which he said looked like an organ but sounded like strings. I haven't been able to track down Philip's reply. Maybe he never bothered.[6]

Other than that, no one knows very much about the *echiquier*, including how to spell it. It also shows up as *eschiquier*, *eschequier*, *eschaquier*, *escacherium*, *exaquir* and, in England, as the *chekkers*. (I don't think it has anything to do with exchequer, meaning finance minister, but the French word *echiquier* also means chessboard, which may explain the English term. Maybe it wasn't an instrument at all, but really a board game.)

The next development in keyboard instruments was the clavichord, a small tabletop rectangular box with the keyboard set into one of the long sides. By depressing a key it gently hits or rubs against a string in the box with a small piece of metal, usually brass, called a tangent, from the Latin *tangere*, meaning "to touch." (Sometimes the term clavier is used to mean specifically the clavichord, but let's not get off on that tangent.)

The clavichord has a lovely tone and its mechanism allows for some subtle variations of the sound, including a kind of vibrato the Germans call *bebung*.[7]

The clavichord became a favorite instrument from the 15th century well into the 17th, admired for its delicacy of tone

---

[5] Edward III's father, Edward II, had been murdered by his wife's lover in a manner that hardly bears repeating. Let's just say it involved a red-hot poker and a certain important lower body orifice.

[6] Philip the Bold was a son of John the Good and a brother of Charles the Wise. In Medieval France you weren't anybody unless you had a fancy nickname.

[7] Beethoven and Chopin call for *bebung* in some of their piano pieces, but they were fooling themselves: you can't do it on a piano.

and intimacy of expression. We're told that King James IV of Scotland entertained his bride, Margaret of England, on their wedding night by playing the lute and the clavichord.[8]

But despite the clavichord's lovely sound, there's not much volume to it. It may be fine for playing by yourself or for a small gathering, but it can't be heard in a large room and it's too easily drowned out by other instruments. What composers wanted was a keyboard instrument with a little more chutzpah.

They found it in the harpsichord, which the French call the *clavecin*, the Italians call the *cembalo* or *clavicembalo* or *gravicembalo* and the Germans call the *Clavicimbel* or sometimes *Kielflügel*.

Instead of rubbing against the string, the harpsichord action plucks the string using a *plectrum*, traditionally made out of the quill of a crow feather or some similar material. (Nowadays, harpsichord builders use plastic or nylon, which I'm sure makes the crows happy.)

In something of a tradeoff, the harpsichord gives a much louder and more decisive sound than the clavichord. That makes it a much better instrument for accompaniment and concert playing, but it's not capable of such subtle expression.

But it seemed to be what Baroque composers were looking for. The harpsichord, which is shaped pretty much like the modern grand piano, though usually smaller (like a horizontal harp, in fact), was the favored instrument of the 16th to 18th centuries in solos, concertos, trio sonatas and other genres. Harpsichords often became quite large and often had two sets of manual keyboards, each with a slightly different sound, and sometimes even a set of pedals like the organ.[9]

Two other types of harpsichord are the spinet, which is smaller and usually roughly triangular, and the virginal, which

---

[8] She may have been disappointed, having had something even more intimate in mind.

[9] Not everybody likes the sound of the harpsichord. English conductor Sir Thomas Beecham once described it as "two skeletons copulating on a corrugated tin roof."

is small, having only one manual keyboard, and rectangular. In 16th-and 17th-century England, the virginal was often referred to in the plural, as a pair of virginals, the way we refer to a pair of scissors. (The name may come because the instrument was considered suitable to be played by young women, who were assumed to be virgins. Others think the instrument may be named after Elizabeth I, the Virgin Queen of England. Personally, I don't believe either of these theories, but you may if you like.)

As in other areas of music, terminology here is a confusing mess — especially in Elizabethan England, where the term virginals was used for almost any sort of stringed keyboard instrument, whether clavichord, harpsichord, spinet, virginal or whatever. Hence such Elizabethan collections now known as *The Fitzwilliam Virginal Book*, which contains nearly 300 short keyboard pieces — pavanes, galliards, preludes, fantasias and more — by such important composers as John Bull, William Byrd, Giles Farnaby, Orlando Gibbons and Thomas Morley.

But towards the end of the Baroque, composers (and listeners) grew tired of the tinny sound of the harpsichord and started looking for an instrument capable of greater expression and dynamic range. Around about 1709, a harpsichord builder in Florence named Bartolomeo Cristofori came up with a harpsichord that, instead of plucking the strings, struck them with little hammers. Because the instrument could sound louder the harder you hit the keys, Cristofori called it a *gravicembalo col piano e forte,* or "harpsichord with soft and loud." Soon other builders began following his example and the piano was born.

Cristofori's *piano e forte* was not exactly an overnight success, but it did begin attracting attention. He and his followers continued tinkering with the insides, changing something here, making an improvement there, until it began to resemble more closely the instrument we call the piano today. They doubled and sometimes tripled the strings to give it more volume and added little gizmos to the mechanism to make it work better.[10]

One of Cristofori's followers in Germany, an organ builder named Gottfried Silbermann, showed a couple of his early pianofortes to J.S. Bach, who wasn't particularly impressed. He considered the sound weak and the mechanism clumsy. Silbermann was a little peeved, but he went back to the drawing board and worked on some improvements.

Bach thought Silbermann's later pianofortes were much better, and when Bach visited King Frederick the Great of Prussia in 1747 he wrote *Das Musikalischer Opfer* ("The Musical Offering"), a set of pieces for Frederick to play on the Silbermann pianoforte the king had just bought. (Actually, he bought a few, just in case one of them broke.)

Evidently Bach wasn't impressed enough with the pianoforte to actually run out and buy one: a catalogue of instruments made at Bach's death in 1750 lists seven harpsichords of various types, a little spinet, three violins, three violas, two cellos, one string bass, a *viola da gamba* and a lute. But no pianos.

Builders continued to modify and improve the pianoforte until they finally came up with the instrument we have today. Among the changes were the addition of a foot pedal that makes the sound softer and another pedal, called the damper pedal, that controls the length of time the sound can continue.

In England (where, you'll recall, they had trouble spelling *sackbut*) there was a short-lived variant called the *fortepiano*, which was not much different from the pianoforte. It didn't last.[11]

The piano's popularity increased in the 18th century, though many diehard traditionalists stuck with the harpsichord, if only for sentimental reasons. The piano really began to take off in the 1770s, when composers such as Mozart and Muzio Clementi (1752-1832) began playing it and writing for it all the time.

[10] Along about 1821, a French builder named Sébastien Erard built a piano with a double escapement. This was considered a big deal.

[11] The modern upright piano is based on the *clavicytherium*, a harpsichord turned on its side that dates back to at least 1511.

By the era of the Romantic composer — Beethoven, Schubert, Schumann, Liszt — the piano had become the most prominent instrument of the day, both for concert virtuosos and for simple family singalongs, and for just about everything in between. The Polish-born French composer Fryderyk (or Frédéric) Chopin (1810-49) wrote almost exclusively for the piano, including piano concertos, piano sonatas, chamber works for piano and strings, and dozens of shorter pieces for solo piano, including *preludes, nocturnes* and little Polish dances called *mazurkas*.

The nocturne is not a specific form but merely a moody piece that's supposed to make you think of night time, which is what the name means. Chopin liked nocturnes: he wrote 19 of them.[12]

Although born in Poland, Chopin moved to Paris as a young man in 1831 and soon became the darling of its flourishing musical and literary society.[13]

From 1838, he shacked up with the French novelist Georges Sand, who was really a woman named Amantine Aurore Lucile Dupin (some of her friends called her Aurore, others called her Lucie) and a baroness in the bargain. Their relationship — during which Chopin wrote many more mazurkas, polonaises, etudes and the like — lasted until about 1847, by which time they were hardly speaking to each other.

After that, Chopin met an English woman named Jane Stirling, who fell madly in love with him and tried to pass herself off as Chopin's wife after he died. Hardly anyone believed her.[14]

Chopin wrote so much music for the piano that in his final years he began to think of himself as one. In another letter to

[12] Most people think Chopin invented the nocturne, but he didn't. The Irish pianist and composer John Field (1782-1837) wrote the first nocturnes and published them in 1814, when Chopin was four years old.

[13] Chopin, we are told, "had the hands of a snake." I'm not sure what that means, but I think it was meant as a compliment.

[14] English women "seem slightly mad," Chopin wrote in a letter to his friend Albert Gryzmala. "They all look at their hands and play wrong notes with sentiment."

a friend, he wrote, "You and I are a couple of old cembalos on which time and circumstances have played out their miserable trills." Chopin, by this time dying of tuberculosis, was all keyed up and strung out, and his illness was putting a damper on his enthusiasm.

The piano has retained its popularity to the present day, although some 20th-century composers, having grown tired of the same old sounds, started looking for new ones. These include banging on the outside of the piano, or strumming across the strings as you would a harp, or shouting into the body of the instrument to make the strings resonate. (If you're going to do this you have to push down on the damper pedal, or it won't work.)

In his 1938 composition *Bacchanal* for piano and dancer, the American composer John Cage (1912-92) introduced what he called a "prepared piano" by adding little pieces of metal, strings, rubber bands and whatnot to the strings, distorting the sound.[15]

The other significant innovation since then has been the invention of the synthesizer, a keyboard instrument that produces all sorts of weird and wonderful sounds electronically. The first synthesizer, patented in 1965, was the Moog synthesizer, named after its American inventor, an electronic engineer named Robert Moog.[16]

A few years later, one of the very first recordings to popularize the sound of the Moog was *Switched-On Bach*, a bunch of Bach reworked for the synthesizer by Walter Carlos.[17]

One of the many virtues of the modern synthesizer is that it can be programmed to imitate the sound of so many other different instruments. It can even sound just like a harpsichord — which is where we started in the first place. Isn't progress wonderful?

[15] The piano may have been prepared for the performance, but I'm not sure the audience was.

[16] If you want to impress your friends, you might point out that Moog should be pronounced to rhyme with "vogue" or "rogue," and not like the sound a cow makes. Nearly everybody gets this wrong.

[17] Walter Carlos is now Wendy Carlos, having been slightly reworked herself.

CHAPTER 15

ORCHESTRAL MANOEUVRES
(IN THE DARK AND OTHERWISE)

THE SYMPHONY, SAYS H.L. Mencken, is "that exact and inevitable form which is the soul of all great music." Unaccustomed as we are to thinking of symphonies as "soul music," this remark may come as a surprise.

The chief virtue of the symphony as a genre, says musicologist Louise Cuyler, is that "it offered serious composers a large, autonomous instrumental form capable of sustaining substantial ideas without recourse to extramusical associations."

And a good thing, too. There's nothing worse for a serious composer than having a whole lot of substantial ideas kicking around the place and nowhere to put them. They clutter up your desk and they just get in the way. (And it's nice not to have to resort to those extramusical associations: too many of them can be harmful to your health.)[1]

The term symphony comes from the Italian *sinfonia*, which means, literally, "sounding together." Baroque Italians (and other Europeans and even the English who wanted to sound Italian because their friends were impressed by that sort of thing) used the term *sinfonia* for just about any piece of music in which a bunch of players were involved. This might be just about anything from the short instrumental introduction of an opera to a sonata or almost any other sort of ensemble work.[2]

---

[1] This is a problem only for "serious" composers, presumably on the theory that non-serious composers don't have any substantial ideas. Or they don't much care where they put them.

[2] Bach used the term *sinfonia* for his three-part keyboard inventions, but that only confuses matters.

Later, the instrumental introduction to an opera or oratorio came to be called an overture, from the Italian *overtura* or the French *ouverture,* both meaning "opening." Early overtures came in two types: the French overture and the Italian overture. (Both the French and Italians are good at making overtures, not all of them having anything to do with music.)

The French overture, favored by Lully and his followers, starts with a stately, pompous introduction followed by a lively contrapuntal section, usually followed by another slow section to finish it off. The overall form, in other words, is slow-fast-slow. Another characteristic of the French overture is the dotted or unequal rhythm that forms the main motive of the opening. Lully was particularly fond of this, maybe because he thought it sounded noble.[3]

The Italian overture, favored by Alessandro Scarlatti and crowd, also has three movements, but in the order fast-slow-fast, similar to the concerto.[4]

For the first half of the 18th century both types were popular, though the Italian overture eventually won out. In fact, it wasn't unusual to find a French overture introducing an Italian opera: Handel liked doing this, just to keep his audiences on their toes. You don't find as many Italian overtures introducing French operas. The French are funny that way.

Early overtures, by the way, usually had nothing much to do with the operas that they introduced: the music was just there to kill time while the people in the audience chatted with some friends, flirted with others and eventually made their way to their seats. (This tradition continued in Italy even into the 19th century. The overture to Rossini's *The Barber Of Seville,* for example, is the same one he'd used for three previous operas. He figured that, since no one was listening anyway, they'd never know the difference.)

[3] Or maybe because, having stubbed his toe too many times, he walked with a limp.

[4] Some scholars argue that the French overture has only two movements, not three, and that the final slower section at the end should not be considered separately. They get pretty hot under the collar if you mention it.

Cesti's opera *Il pomo d'oro,* written in 1667, is one of the first in which the music of the overture actually has anything to do with the rest of the opera. But even he was ahead of his time: it took about another century for many other composers to catch on to this trick. In the 1770s and '80s, Gluck used the overture to set the mood for the opening scene, a practice later adopted by Mozart, Wagner and others.[5]

It wasn't until the 19th century that composers such as Rossini and Meyerbeer started using the overture as a kind of grab-bag of the opera's hit tunes — a practice that continues to this day in Broadway-style musicals.

And what does all this have to do with the symphony, you ask? Well, everything, as it turns out.

The symphony is an 18th-century development that combines little bits of the *sinfonia* and overture (mostly Italian, but with a dash of French thrown in, just for flavor), the solo concerto, the sonata (*da chiesa, da camera,* the *trio sonata* and the solo sonata), the dance suite, the *concerto grosso* and a few other trends and genres, all rolled up into one neat package.[6]

"The symphony," as Cuyler puts it, "might be seen as a magnet that, by the middle of the eighteenth century, was attracting every important development in instrumental music into its field." We can picture the 18th-century symphonist sitting at his desk, scraping off the iron filings and plucking loose nails or stray bits of metal from his waistcoat.

Beethoven, we are told, had a magnetic personality obviously from all that energy he put into writing his symphonies.

Nowadays we use the term symphony to mean both the musical genre and the ensemble that performs it. The ensemble or group itself is also called an orchestra. Or, to be doubly sure,

---

[5] Gluck's *Iphegénie en Tauride* overture sets up a nifty thunderstorm for the opening scene.

[6] Some musicologists maintain it is impossible to trace the development of the symphony without discussing the important contributions of the *style galant,* the *Empfindsamer Stil* and the *Sturm und Drang movement.* Just watch me.

a symphony orchestra.[7]

Sometimes, orchestras are called *Philharmonic* orchestras, from a fancy Latin term meaning "love of harmony." Considering some of the music these groups play (and the way they are run) the description is not entirely accurate.

The symphonic form got its most important start in the early 18th century with a group of composers known as the Mannheim School, because they were associated with the court of Karl Theodor, who was the Elector of Pfalzbayern and a pretty good guy all around.[8]

Karl Theodor had gathered together an ensemble of terrific musicians, including such composer-players as Franz Xavier Richter (1709-89), Ignaz Holzbauer (1711-83), Johann Stamitz (1717-57) and Christian Cannabich (1731-98). It was a small orchestra of 25 to 30 or so, mostly strings with pairs of flutes, oboes and French horns. There weren't very many in the group, but they played well. Charles Burney called it "an army of generals."[9]

This Mannheim School made many important changes in musical style. They replaced the harpsichord *basso continuo* of the Baroque by writing out the accompaniment in the lower string instruments and gave most of the important tunes to the violins — a mistake that generally continues to this day. (There was no conductor and since there was now no harpsichord the players were led by the first violinist, which is where we get the tradition of the concertmaster.)[10]

The Mannheim movement has been called "the cradle of the symphony" because so many important musical ideas were present in their infancy.

---

[7] We never refer to the music itself as an orchestra. It just isn't done.

[8] This group of composers is sometimes referred to as the *Pfalzbayrische Schule*, or Pfalzbayern School, but only by musical snobs.

[9] Burney had his faults, but he was handy with a metaphor.

[10] It was Stamitz who got the bright idea of having all the string players move their bows the same direction at the same time. Before that it was pretty haphazard, and you might find yourself getting poked in the eye.

Some, in fact, were pretty juvenile. Among these were the frequent use (or overuse) of a rapid ascending theme, known as "the Mannheim rocket," a big tremolo in the upper violins, known as "the Mannheim roll," and a gradual crescendo for full orchestra, known as "the Mannheim steamroller." Whatever else it might have had, the orchestra had a great marketing department.

Probably the most influential of these composers was Johann Stamitz, whose work was carried on by his sons Karl and Anton. By the time Johann Stamitz took over the Mannheim orchestra in 1745, one historian tells us, "most of the symphony's teething troubles were well under control." Now it was time to move on to toilet training.

Mannheim wasn't the only centre of symphonic writing in the early 1700s: composers in other centres, such as Johann Adolph Hasse (1699-1783), J.S. Bach's son C.P.E. Bach (1714-88), Giovanni Battista Sammartini (1701-75) and Georg Matthias Monn (1717-50) were likewise playing around with symphonic form. It was just that Mannheim had all the catchy nicknames.

Most of the symphonies of this period, by the way, had only three movements, the same fast-slow-fast of the Italian overture and the concerto. But Monn, for one, would occasionally throw in a fourth movement when nobody was looking. He liked to live dangerously.

Haydn and Mozart made the next big changes to the symphony, formalizing the *sonata allegro form* for the first movement and adding a lilting minuet before the final movement. Mozart wrote about 41 symphonies (and every one a gem), while Haydn — who was older and had more time — wrote more than a hundred.[11]

Because he wrote so many of them, many of Haydn's symphonies have cutesy nicknames, not all of which come from the composer himself. But they do help us keep track.

Many of the nicknames have fanciful stories attached. The

[11] Most reference books will say 104, but the latest count seems to be about 107 or even 108. Anyway, more than a hundred.

Surprise Symphony (No. 94, in G) gets its name from the big chord that comes crashing in on the first movment. ("This will startle the ladies," Haydn said.) The *Farewell Symphony* (No. 45, in F-sharp minor) has a joke at the end, where players leave the orchestra one by one, leaving only two to finish. It was Haydn's subtle way of letting his patron, Prince Nicholaus Esterhazy, know it was time to go home. (As each player left the stage he snuffed out his candle, leading to what you might call orchestral manoeuvres in the dark. Nowadays we don't use candles, we do it with an electric light orchestra.)

Other nicknames include "Oxford," "London," "The Bear" and "The Hen." Haydn was not only prolific, he was inventive. In fact, says biographer Rosemary Hughes, he was "the father of the symphony."[12]

If Haydn was the father of the symphony, Beethoven was its wayward son. Although he "forged the connecting link between the classicists and the romanticists," Beethoven was not about to be chained down by any niceties of formal structure.

Even his very first symphony, *Symphony No. 1*, Opus 21, although ostensibly in C major — a nice, safe, conventional key — opens not in the home key but in F major, with side trips through A minor and G major before finally settling into C major as it should. Worse than that, the symphony opens on a dominant-seventh chord, which is the instrumental equivalent of starting a choral piece with "Amen." Clearly, Beethoven wasn't about to meekly follow the rules, although after the risky opening the symphony calms down considerably.

Beethoven wrote only nine symphonies, which may not seem very many when compared to the output of Haydn or Mozart or others of that generation. But what he lacked in quantity, Beethoven made up for in quality. Beethoven symphonies are passionate, expressive, and chock-full of drama. In most of them, he replaced the third-movement minuet of the

---

[12] He was also, you'll recall, "the father of the string quartet." He sure got around. No wonder they called him "Papa" Haydn.

earlier Classical composers with the scherzo, which he felt was more expressive.[13]

Originally an admirer of Napoleon, Beethoven had planned to dedicate his third symphony to the French general, until he found out that Napoleon had proclaimed himself emperor, whereupon he tore up the title page inscribed "Buonaparte" in a fit of anger. He later called it his *Eroica*, or "Heroic" Symphony.

Or so says Beethoven's friend and pupil Ferdinand Ries, who claims to have been in the room when it happened. I'm not about to argue, and besides, it makes a great story.[14]

One of Beethoven's important contributions to the genre was to expand both the size and the range of the orchestra, by adding more instruments, including piccolos for the high notes and contra-bassoons for the low ones. By the time he got to his Ninth Symphony, Beethoven made the orchestra even bigger by adding soloists and a whole choir in the fourth movement.

The finale of the Ninth is a huge, dramatic moment, a setting for orchestra and singers of Friedrich von Schiller's *Ode An Die Freude*, or "Ode To Joy."[15] The Ninth had its first performance on May 7, 1824 with the composer conducting, and the crowd loved it. Beethoven, by this time completely deaf, had no idea until one of the soloists took him by the arm and turned him around to see the audience applauding and waving handkerchiefs. That performance made some money but a repeat two weeks later lost at the box office. No one ever said great art makes great money.

After Beethoven, composers continued writing symphonies, though none with quite so much conviction. Some of them seem just to be going through the motions. Symphonies of the Romantic era and afterwards may be bigger, longer and more

---

[13] Beethoven was no dancer: his legs were short and stubby and he was just plain clumsy all around.

[14] Some people mistake the title *Eroica* with "Erotica." That would be something else again.

[15] *Freude*, in this case, has nothing to do with Sigmund Freud and his theories of psychoanalysis. There's little joy to be found in Freud.

emotional than Beethoven's, but they don't necessarily say much more than his.

Franz Schubert wrote 8½ symphonies, his sketches for the last two movements of his *Unfinished Symphony,* No. 8, having apparently been permanently misplaced by his friend Anselm Hüttenbrenner one day in 1822.[16]

Tchaikovsky wrote six symphonies, which although lovely are hardly startling. Johannes Brahms managed to write four symphonies, having been rather sidetracked by his *Requiem.* Hector Berlioz wrote only half as many as Brahms, though his *Symphonie fantastique* does have five movements. He wrote it after falling in love with Harriet Smithson, an Irish actress playing Shakespeare's Ophelia. The story even has a happy ending: Berlioz met Smithson two years later and they were married in 1832.

Later composers have expanded the form in various ways, if only just to fool around. Gustav Mahler's *Symphony No. 8* in E-flat major (1907) is known as the "Symphony of a Thousand," though one of the few performances, in Liverpool Cathedral in 1965, used only 700 performers — 520 singers and a choir of 180.[17] The *Sinfonia Antarctica* of English composer Ralph Vaughan Williams (No. 7, 1953) calls for orchestra and wind machine. (That's a wind machine separate from the conductor.)[18]

In addition to writing six symphonies, the American composer George Antheil (1900-59) wrote detective stories, a medical treatise on the glandular problems of criminals and a daily newspaper column of advice to the lovelorn. Well, there's more to life than writing symphonies, you know.

---

[16] Alexander Borodin wrote an *Unfinished Symphony*, too, but his isn't nearly so famous. After all, Schubert had thought of it first.

[17] I wonder if anyone in the audience asked for a refund?

[18] Canadian composer R. Murray Schafer has written a concert piece, not exactly a symphony, for orchestra and snowmobile. It's an interesting effect, but only if the snowmobile is in tune.

CHAPTER

CODA

LET'S TAKE A MOMENT now, just for fun, and look at the history of tonality in classical music in terms of socio-political theories. Well, why not? Just think of it as a free thesis topic, in case you were looking for one.

The Medieval and Renaissance period was obviously a theocracy, in which the rules of both melody and harmony were established by each note's relationship to God and by a lot of heavy-duty regulations set down by the Church, under what it considered to be divine authority.

After that, in the 18th and 19th centuries, came a kind of oligarchy, in which harmonic tonality was controlled by a handful of notes and by their close relatives. In the major-minor tonality of the Baroque and Classic and even Romantic eras, the tonic chord or key rules as a king, the dominant as the prince and heir apparent. All the others — the sub-dominant, the mediant and the rest — have their rightful places as earls, dukes, barons and so on down the peerage.[1]

The 20th century has seen several attempts at disrupting this established social order. Not all of them succeeded — in fact, none of them has completely — but you have to give composers points for trying.

Serialism, which we might think of as Schoenberg's attempt at musical socialism — in which each note is equally

---

[1] This entire system is very sexist, but that's a whole different story.

important and all notes are employed — works better in theory than in practice.[2]

It may have been necessary to free the musical proletariat from the oppressive shackles of rigid tonality, but complete atonality too often dissolves into chaos. (Or, in the case of strict Schoenbergian serialism, you've just traded oligarchy for dictatorship, which I'm not sure is any better.)

John Cage and others have experimented with tonal systems based on rolling dice or other random elements. This method, known as *aleatoric* or chance music (not to be confused with musical chants), is a form of anarchy, with no rules at all. It tends to be just about as productive.

To avoid these failings, some composers have turned (or returned) to alternative tonalities, borrowing elements here and there from ancient modality or from other cultures pretty much however they felt like it. Many composers established tonalities peculiar to themselves, or sometimes peculiar only to an idividual work. It's a sort of musical libertarianism, if you will.

The musical-political climate nowadays seems to be all over the map. Who knows where it might lead? Maybe to a new world order. Dvorak has already given us a *New World Symphony*.

---

[2] So does real socialism, come to that.

THE AUTHOR

If It Ain't Baroque ... is David W. Barber's fourth book of musical humor for Sound And Vision. He feels he's finally getting the hang of it. Barber lives in Westport, Ontario., where he is a freelance writer, and proprietor of White Knight Bookstore. In his non-existent free time, Barber enjoys kayaking and canoeing, blending tea and the challenge of continual home renovations. He is also a freelance performer and composer whose works include two symphonies, chamber and choral works and numerous vocal-jazz arrangements.

THE ILLUSTRATOR

Dave Donald can't remember when he didn't scrawl his little marks on most surfaces, so it doesn't come as much of a surprise that he now makes a living doing just that. He is currently balancing a steady job as art director for a Toronto magazine publisher with his other more abstruse pursuits. This book represents Dave's fourth illustrative collaboration with David Barber.

Also by David Barber and Dave Donald

A MUSICIAN'S DICTIONARY (1983)
ISBN 0-920151-03-5

BACH, BEETHOVEN, AND THE BOYS (1986)
Music History As It Ought To Be Taught
ISBN 0-920151-07-8

WHEN THE FAT LADY SINGS (1990)
Opera History As It Ought
ISBN 0-920151-11-6

GETTING A HANDEL ON MESSIAH (1994)
ISBN 0-920151-17-5

by Dave Donald

HECTOR AND THE BIG HOUSE (1977)

If It Ain't Baroque...
More Music History As
It Ought To Be Taught

First Published in Canada by

SOUND AND VISION
359 RIVERDALE AVENUE
TORONTO CANADA M4J 1A4

First printing **September, 1992**

15 13 11 9 7 5	- printings -	6 8 10 12 14
99 97	- year -	96 98

Canadian Cataloguing in Publication Data

Barber, David W. 1958–
If it ain't baroque : more music history as
it ought to be taught
Includes bibliographical references.

ISBN 0-920151-15-9

1. Music - Humor. 1. Donald, David C. 11. Title.
ML65.B37 1992   780'.207   C92-095054-X

Typeset in ITC New Baskerville
Printed and bound in Canada on acid free paper